Missionary Man

Missionary Man

§

Billy Gray
&
Trista Plantholt

Dedication

God has favored me by letting me pastor a church: The Gathering. Its members chose me, a layman, over far more qualified personnel.

My penchant has always been that of a plebeian; however, The Gathering is a highly sophisticated, affluent church body that understands the call on my life for missions. I am at liberty to spend as much time as God dictates away from the church with its blessings and with its support.

To the church body, and to the staff: David Seering, Jay Stone, Ann Stone, and certain other members, I dedicate this humble transcription to you. God bless!

Contents

Acknowledgments

§

MISSIONARY MAN IS A COMPILATION of love stories that take place across five continents. Although you can hear the cries of pain, sickness, and hardships in some of these stories, ultimately the crescendo of victory is the sweet note they end on.

There is no reward this side of heaven as sweet as sharing Jesus with the lost. When they accept and you see the metamorphosis in their lives, it's more thrilling than a hole in one.

So, why write such a book of stories? Well, first, to encourage others to be obedient to the "great commission" (Mark 16:15).

Second, I began realizing that people like Mother Teresa, Annie Armstrong, and Dr. Livingston were people just like us, with a call from God on their lives. They got tired, wept, prayed, and persevered.

Not everyone is called to the mission field full time; there are many opportunities on a short-term basis, both at home and abroad.

You say, "I can't go." Then give, so others can go. You say, "I can't give"? Then pray for those who can go and can give.

So, I'll see you in Africa, Saint Kitts, India, or maybe at the local gas station as we hand out tracts to enlist the lost.

What say you?

CHAPTER 1
Gambia

§

THIS WAS MY FIRST TRIP to Africa, and I was excited to see what Gambia had to offer.

After a little research, I discovered that Gambia was the smallest country in Africa. However, 1.3 million people lived within these small borders. The population was 95 percent Muslim. Gambia's dominant ethnic group, the Mandingo, was made famous by Alex Haley's book, *Roots*. Half of Gambia's gross national product came from tourism, mostly that of Europeans, who flocked there because it was an inexpensive and pleasant place to visit. Gambia's climate is a pleasant eighty degrees in the daytime and sixty degrees at night.

Gambia is an English-speaking country; however, its dialect can be very hard to understand, which caused us some confusion while trying to rent a van from the airport. After a little patience and persistence, our thirteen-member team piled into one and took a three-hour ride to the hotel.

The entrance to the hotel was at the end of a long dirt road, with four expressionless armed guards posted in front of the nine-foot iron gates. These guys would have intimidated Goliath.

I had received my assignment to the largest church in Gambia, the Glory Baptist Fellowship Church in Banjul. Banjul is the capital and has the greatest density of population.

I was told that our movements within the country would be limited due to government issues as well as for our own safety. We were instructed to be back at the compound by sunset; otherwise, our safety could not be guaranteed.

After supper, I ventured down to the Atlantic Ocean to stretch my legs on the beach, which was about half a mile from our compound. The beach was wide, with dirty-white sand. Even though it was late afternoon, the beach was still fairly crowded, mostly with Africans and also some Europeans. The African women were covered, but the European women were topless.

Immediately, I was hustled by a hawker, selling black-and-white beads on a flimsy string. I politely declined his initial sales pitch, though he became much more forceful. He accused me of being an American who did not like blacks and questioned why I was even in his country. He aggressively went on to explain that the black-and-white beads symbolized unity between the two races; purchasing a bracelet would show my love of all humankind.

Tension filled the air. The vendor's disdain for this foreign white man grew. I realized that this would be how many locals would view me. I reassured him of my benevolence toward all races and purchased a bracelet for a dollar.

I headed back to the compound, realizing my need to stay within the boundaries while alone. As I was walking, a strikingly gorgeous Gambian woman began strolling next to me. She asked, "How are you?" Her voice was as smooth as satin, barely above a whisper. She was so close to me, I could feel her body heat and smell her sweet perfume. She was full figured in all the right places and lean in the other ones. Her attire left little to the imagination.

She added, "Would you like some company tonight, or maybe a massage?" Her soft, sultry voice soothed my ears; her aroma was intoxicating, and her presence was alluring. She persisted in trying to entice me with her provocative ways. We approached the boundaries of my compound, which she was not allowed to cross.

I stopped. I looked into her honey-brown eyes for the first time. She had small facial features, high cheekbones, a timid smile with pearly-white teeth, and lips as red as a rose. I took her chin into my hand and paused for a moment, looking deeply into her eyes. She eagerly awaited my proposi-tion. I asked, "Young lady, are you a Christian?"

Repulsed by my question, she recoiled and said, "No, I'm a Muslim."

"May I share the truth of Jesus Christ with you?" I asked.

She looked at me with disgust. She turned and fled from me as swiftly as she had sidled up.

Grateful to have escaped my journey down to the beach, I praised God for His protection and deliverance. Needless to say, I did not go back to the beach alone while on this trip.

The next morning, the hotel provided us with a delicious breakfast and sent us on our way with a sack lunch. While passing through the crowded town of Banjul, I understood why we had been given a sack lunch. Meats and fish were openly displayed on vendors' tables with no ice or refrigeration. The flies were so prevalent that it was hard to discern what kind of meat was on display. The odor was atrocious. It was a wonder that retching was not far behind.

Pedestrians crowded the sidewalks and the streets while the vehicles just inched along. It was impossible to walk without being jostled. We were in the perfect setting for people with sticky fingers; we remained constantly vigilant.

At Glory Baptist Fellowship Church, I met my interpreter, the music minister, Emmanuel Karlya. He spoke fluent English and played several instruments proficiently. He told me he was a refugee from a war-torn town in Liberia.

There had been no schedule or appointments set for us, so our plan was to propagate house to house, in the streets, and within businesses.

The Christians I met were lovely, delightful people. They were not intimidated by their Muslim counterparts; they were bold and courageous in sharing the truth of Christ.

Emmanuel and I visited bars, cafes, beauty shops, restaurants, and clothing stores. Sometimes we witnessed to the owners, and other times to the employees. On three occasions, an owner brought friends in to hear our story of salvation.

Witnessing to individuals was immensely rewarding; it was a time to feel the pulse of the person. Word began to spread, doors opened, and hearts were receptive to the call of the Holy Spirit. Groups of people came to hear us witness.

We were led to several home churches to share; people gave their hearts to Christ. I realized that my mission was not only to the lost but also to encourage and embolden the faithful.

In God's perfect timing, we were in Gambia during the Festival of Sacrifice, Eid al-Adha, high holy days for Muslims. The ceremony represented two Islamic events: the pilgrimage to Mecca and Ibrahim's (Abraham's) willingness to obey Allah's command to sacrifice Ismail (Ishmael). All came to bring a blood sacrifice to cleanse their sins away—the rich and the poor, the upper class and the lower class.

According to Islamic teaching, the command to Ibrahim was made to test his obedience to Allah. Just as Ibrahim's hand was raised to sacrifice Ismail, Allah stopped him and provided a ram in the boy's stead. Ibrahim's act of obedience was commemorated by the sacrifice of an animal, such as a lamb, sheep, goat, cow, or camel. The meat was then divided into three parts, with equal portions given to the family, to friends, and to the poor.

Christians, Jews, and Muslims, each refer to Abraham as the father of their religion. The division is according to each of Abraham's two sons, Isaac and Ishmael. According to Genesis 15:22, God promised Abraham and Sarah a son, but after many years of waiting. Sarah feared she would not provide Abraham with the heir that God had promised, so she took matters into her own hands. She offered her handmaiden, Hagar, to Abraham. Hagar gave birth to Ishmael.

Thirteen years after Ishmael was born, Sarah finally conceived and gave birth to Isaac. According to the Bible, Isaac was the chosen son that God had promised to Abraham, and Ishmael was the illegitimate son. However, the Muslims teach that Ishmael was the chosen son.

I arrived to the event by a cab. The four-person vehicle had six people stuffed within. The cabbie did not let this deter him from also picking up a woman holding a goat. In order for us to accommodate Goat Lady and her animal, a rotund woman had to sit on my lap. We were all profusely sweating, and the odor was horrendous; the air was hot and stale. The only air circulation we had was from a slightly open window.

When we arrived at Goat Lady's destination, a huge argument ensued as she gave the cabbie his fare. The debate was whether she had to pay for two passengers or one. She believed she only owed for one, but he insisted that she owed the goat's fare as well. They finally compromised; she gave him a fare and a half.

I took this opportunity to exit the cab after heaving Rotund Lady off of my lap, opting to walk the remainder of the way.

Upon approaching the celebration area, I saw holding pens retaining animals brought to be slaughtered. The most prevalent were goats. Their throats were slit and blood poured out. It was indeed a gruesome and bloody sight to behold.

I saw no joy on the faces of the devout Muslims. This event was nothing more than a yearly ordeal or task for them to perform. It was the complete opposite of receiving atonement from Jesus Christ's shed blood, which offers joy and peace. "He is the atoning sacrifice for our sins, and not only for our sins, but also for the sins of the whole world" (1 John 2:2). The blood of animals sprinkled on the sinner only cleanses outwardly. But the blood of Christ cleanses us internally and externally (Hebrews 9:13–14).

The following day, I visited a large school in Banjul operated by the Baptist church. A lady rancher from Texas, and I had been invited to minister in the school. I found it unbelievable that I was in a Muslim country, invited to preach the Gospel in a school, and allowed to pray publicly with the students, yet I could not do this in the United States, which claims to be under God.

I told the students the story of the birth, life, crucifixion, and resurrection of our Savior, Jesus Christ. I also told them of Noah, King David, and Daniel. I asked them to raise their hands if they wanted to accept Jesus as their Lord and Savior. Most hands rose, and I led the interested in a sinner's prayer.

Several adults prayed with us as well. The security guard, Babaucarr Dampha from the Wolof tribe, sat in the shadows, listening intently with a big grin on his face. He was the most eager to pray the sinner's prayer. What a treat!

Since we were confined to the compound at night, our host, Dennis, always arranged some form of entertainment for us after dinner. Jugglers tossed up sharp or fiery objects as though they were cushy balls, acrobats flipped this way and bent that way, dancers moved and gyrated to the African beat. Each night offered a unique entertainment from individuals from different African tribes.

After the entertainment concluded, our team would meet in a semi-circle where we shared the day's events and ended with a prayer. There was something awe inspiring about praying under the black-velvet African sky dotted with bright twinkling stars. So many stars, it was as though I could reach up and grab one right out of the sky. Only a masterful Creator could do that. Our Comforter dwelt among us and surrounded us with His blissful warmth.

I longed to reach out beyond the boundaries given to me. I made a request to visit the prison, but the government refused my appeal.

During some of my excursions, I noticed an island, Barra, serviced by a ferry. I told Emmanuel that I wanted to go to Barra. Emmanuel explained that the ferry was very dangerous. It was often overcrowded, making it easy for pickpockets to prey on victims. The previous week, a ferry had sunk, and the majority of passengers had drowned. Nevertheless, he agreed to accompany me on the ferry.

We paid our toll and were ushered into a small room. This tiny space was standing room only. We were crammed in like crayons in a crayon box, bodies against bodies.

Emmanuel's eyes never left me. I was the only white man in the group of five hundred passengers. For the first time in my life, I understood the uncomfortable feeling of being the minority.

After a suffocating forty minutes of waiting and breathing the exhaled air of others, we finally boarded the ferry. The boat was no different than the waiting room, in the sense that it was standing room only; however, it had an open deck above the lower, enclosed deck. Emmanuel and I made our way inside the lower level and waited for the remainder of the passengers to board.

As the ferry departed, I felt unfamiliar hands at my backside. Instantly, I knew that I was feeling the nimble fingers of a pickpocket. I slapped the hand away, and two men shouted at me as though I was at fault for something.

Immediately, Emmanuel turned, and with a fierce look on his face like that of a momma bear protecting her cub from a mountain lion, he growled loud enough for everyone to turn our way and shouted, "I am a warrior from Liberia. This man of God is in my charge. If you harm him, you have harmed me, and I will have no choice but to kill you!"

However, this did not dissuade the two pickpockets from trying to coerce the crowd to favor them over a Liberian and a white man. The crowd was initially on the side of the thieves, yelling that a white man had no business slapping the hand of an innocent African man.

Emmanuel continued to stare down at these two criminals with such a ferocious look that the crowd grew completely silent. The men threatened to "take care of us" as soon as the boat docked.

Emmanuel responded, "You have heard my position, so be prepared to die."

This all happened so fast, it seemed surreal. I was caught off guard by this side of Emmanuel that I had never seen before. I knew him as an intelligent, musically inclined, godly, kind, and helpful man. But the look of intensity in his eyes proved that he had another aspect that happened to come in handy at that moment. I was just glad I was on his good side.

Emmanuel suggested we go up to the top deck to get some fresh air. The crowd parted way as if paying homage to a conquering hero.

The River Gambia ferry, loaded with 498 passengers, trucks, cars, goats, groceries, one Liberian warrior, and one white man, glided across the placid emerald water to Barra. My soul was at peace; I knew God had sent me a protector, and his name was Emmanuel: "God with us." We never saw those men again.

We celebrated the closing rally at the Glory Baptist Fellowship Church. All the attendees were dressed in their finest attire. Women were in wide-brimmed hats with dresses to match, and men wore vibrantly colored suits and ties. The church was overflowing with people; all the floor seats were taken as well as those in the balcony. People were standing in the isles; the foyer doors were opened so that those standing out there could participate.

Emmanuel started the music by beating his drum and then other musicians joined in. The music had that wonderful, melodious African sound; the singers' voices were deep and rich. We praised and worshipped our Lord in such an awesome, heartfelt, and powerful way that I could feel the floor vibrating while shouts of joy reverberated off the walls, and my spirit leapt to the beat.

All the team members came to the pulpit and gave their testimony, sharing the victories God had given them in Africa. One team member shared that a ninety-year-old man had asked God for forgiveness just before he took his last breath. Many had stories of drunks putting down the drink and of marriages restored. On and on the stories went as the team shared the miracles of God in these people's lives.

When my turn came, I stood up on the high platform overlooking all the beautiful people. They were resplendent, because the Holy Spirit was reigning supreme within their hearts. I felt as though I could give an invitation without even preaching, because the presence of the Lord was so evident.

I gave a short message on the glorious grace of God and His unending love. The message was received enthusiastically, and people poured down the aisles, seeking repentance, salvation, and restored relationships. It was such a sight to behold, I was overwhelmed. There were hours of hugging, crying, praying, and praising.

This trip was so spirit filled and the people were so wonderful that I hated for it to end. But it had to, as all things must.

I heard the voice of the Lord saying, "Whom shall I send and who will go for us?" Then I said, "Here am I, send me!" (Isaiah 6:8)

People getting off the ferry

Emmanuel the interpreter; Billy Gray; and
Babaucarr Dampha, the security guard

CHAPTER 2

Guadeloupe

§

THIS WAS MY FIRST TRIP to Guadeloupe. Along with me were three lady friends in their seventies, taking their first mission trip. These ladies had a love for the Lord and were ready for the challenge.

And a challenge this trip proved to be; this was not one in which we had prearranged appointments. No, this mission called for cold calling, which meant stopping people in the streets to witness, or knocking on strangers' doors to share Christ. This was no easy task and not for the faint of heart.

Guadeloupe is a French West Indies island located between Puerto Rico and Venezuela. Summertime in Guadeloupe is very hot and humid, akin to Florida in the dog days of August. Though Guadeloupe is a French-speaking place, there are some English-speaking churches as well.

We worked with two churches: Pointe-a-Pitre and Gosier. The members were English speaking Dominicans who had immigrated to Guadeloupe.

Church services lasted about three hours. The music was loud and rhythmic, and the people were jubilant and vibrant. I overheard a church member say, "These white ladies are good Christians, but they ain't got no rhythm." Fortunately, rhythm isn't a requirement for serving the Lord.

Each night, we held services in both churches. We were amazed at the huge turnouts. Those who did not arrive early enough to get in willingly listened outside the open windows.

The people were hospitable and energetic. We discovered that the central parts of their lives and their primary source of socializing were going to work and attending church. Most of the members were blue-collar workers in construction, doing tile, bricks, or plumbing.

All these people had a great interest in their government. Since 1974, Guadeloupe has been represented in the French parliament. The citizens voted in the French election and received medical care from the French government.

Marge, a beloved lady friend who accompanies me on many island trips, described a memorable event: Long before the service began, the church was alive with joyous, ringing music, with ladies singing on stage moving to the rhythm. Each one was wearing a colorful, long-sleeved dress and a wonderfully large hat decked out with matching ribbons, flowers, and bows. A very well-dressed man joined the ladies on stage after parking his black Jaguar safely at the back door.

Once the service was in full swing, the entire congregation sang loudly, swaying to the beat of the music. A tiny, aged, white-haired lady was animatedly dancing in front of the stage. When the pastor delivered his message, everyone listened and accompanied him with many hearty cries of, "Amen, Brother!"

The church was full; however, there was one person missing. The pastor told us of a faithful choir member who had been bedridden and unable to attend services. After the service, we decided to visit her unannounced.

We walked up the dirt road to the small house, which was neat and tidy. Through the front door, we could see a grand, immaculate bed; on it was sitting a nicely dressed, large woman, perhaps fifty years old. It was obvious that she could not move from her bed.

As we went inside, the woman spoke to a small boy who was outside the window next to her bed. She handed him some money to run an errand. This was clearly an arrangement that suited them both.

I approached her. In one hand, she held her Bible; with the other, she held on to my hand. She paid close attention as we spoke of the glories of Jesus Christ. She affirmed her commitment to live a life of one in Christ, as a certain believer. She thanked us for visiting, smiled, and said with misty eyes, "I knew that you were coming." The Lord's messengers must have informed her, because we had not even known.

Thankfully, Marge speaks fluent French, because one day we were asked to speak to an elderly couple who only spoke that language. Her linguistic skills and the power of the Lord brought this couple to salvation.

After three days of walking under the hot sun, I was looking forward to having my turn in the one car shared among the four teams. Just as I stepped to get into it with my guide, I heard, "Wait! I want him to go with me." I felt a jolt in my spine, because I was the only "him" there.

I turned to see that the voice belonged to an attractive, light-skinned lady about thirty years old. She was tall, lean, and very well proportioned. She was wearing tight jeans, knee-high, black-leather boots with six-inch spiked heels, a sheer white shirt, and a biker's cap to top it off.

She introduced me to her entourage which consisted of a mentally challenged teenage boy, a seventeen-year-old girl, and a lady large enough to be a wrestler with her five-year-old son. There was no doubt that Biker Babe was calling the shots in this group. She turned to me and said, "Come on. We have a long walk ahead." And off we went.

The farther we walked, the seedier the neighborhood became. We walked under a train trestle where the winos were lounging in the shade, escaping the heat. The catcalls, whistles, and remarks from onlookers grew more frequent the deeper into the neighborhood we walked. I could not understand the French words, but I could imagine what they were saying.

Biker Babe was resolute. She held her head up high, eyes straight ahead, as she continued walking with determination. We walked up a hill with lush, green grass. Some people reclined on the lawn while others enjoyed a picnic at some tables. Behind this pastoral setting was set a three-story hospital. "We must stop here," said the woman.

Thinking this was our destination, we followed her through the entire first floor of the building as she peeked her head into each room and then moved on. Then we proceeded to the second floor.

"Are we visiting someone in particular? I can ask for help," I said, wondering what she was doing.

"God will tell us when we have the right room," she answered matter of factly. I began wondering, *Is this lady a lunatic? What is going on here?*

Moments later, we walked into a room, where she told the thirty-something man lying in the bed, "You need to hear what this man has to say. Period!"

I asked Biker Babe, "What is his name?"

She responded, "I've never seen this man before. But God says you need to talk to him."

The man in the bed and I had something in common: neither of us understood what was happening, but we were unwilling to oppose Biker Babe's commands.

We introduced ourselves; he told me he was dying from cirrhosis of the liver and was uncertain of his eternal destination. I attempted to explain salvation to him in the simplest of terms, beginning with, "All people are sinners."

He willingly admitted that he was a sinner. His life had been marred by alcohol abuse. The love of his life had divorced him. He had literally drunk himself to death and lost everything.

I continued, "Jesus died on the cross to save you from your sins. First, admit you are a sinner. Then, believe that Jesus died on the cross to save you from your sins, and on the third day, He arose from the grave. Trust Him as your Savior, and you will be saved. You can have assurance that you will have a home in heaven upon your last breath here on earth."

He grabbed hold of the concept like a drowning man grabbing a life preserver. We prayed the sinner's prayer together. The man whispered into Biker Babe's ear, "Hand me my shirt hanging on the nail on the wall over there."

She complied. He pulled out a five-dollar bill and said, "This is all the money I have left in this world. Please give it to the reverend."

I was embarrassed and stunned, "No, sir, I do not do this for money."

Biker Babe leaned over to me and said, "You will offend him if you don't take the money." So I took it and later gave it to the church.

A peace that surpassed all understanding was present on this dying man's face. He now had assurance of a home in paradise with a perfect body, in the presence of a loving, forgiving, healing Savior. I was mesmerized and astounded at how awesome God was and how He had orchestrated this event just in time.

It was apparent to me that God was using Biker Babe for His glory. A woman the world would call a "sex symbol," He was using as His guide for me to follow. I followed obediently. It is amazing how God works and whom He uses.

We ventured back to the street, down to the ghetto, the entire entourage following Biker Babe. Empty and broken wine bottles littered the landscape. Boarded-up houses, broken windows, and ragged, dirty children surrounded us. There was nothing bucolic or lovely about this place. In fact, apprehension would have eaten at my emotions if I had not been with Biker Babe.

Finally, we came to a closed-off alley that had only one way in and one way out. At the end of the alley, there sat two cars on jacks and one motorcycle. Three mammoth men wearing sleeveless shirts and covered in tattoos were working on the cars, while one small guy was tinkering with the motorcycle.

With the assurance of Alexander the Great, Biker Babe marched up to these mountain-sized men, pointed at the biggest, meanest-looking guy, who was obviously the leader, and said to me, "This is the guy you need to talk to."

Looking back at the mechanic, she said, "Joe, you need to hear what this man has to say."

Sheepishly, he agreed. "Go ahead, sir."

Biker Babe held up her hand as if to stop me and said, "Don't you have any manners? Invite this man of God into your house so he doesn't have to stand in this filthy alley."

Embarrassed, Joe invited our "godly gang" into his home. Two other men followed, joining us at the large dining-room table. The little guy stood in the alley with his head poked through the open window.

Biker Babe started things out by saying, "What this man says is true. He is concerned about where you are going to spend eternity. I've been hearing him preach at the church. He's fo' real. So you'd better listen up!"

Sitting directly across from Joe, I began telling him, "Anyone can drink, smoke, fight, mistreat women, and be abusive toward society, but it takes a real man to follow Christ. It takes a strong man to stand up for his convictions and a courageous man to live for God in the face of adversity."

I told Joe that Jesus paid a price that he could not pay for himself or strong arm out of anyone else. "Jesus died for you. If you accept His free gift of salvation, you will gain His strength and courage and a home in heaven. But it will cost you all you have: your very life."

The furrows on the men's brows softened, their eyes became gentler, and their demeanor was more pleasing. The more I spoke, the more each man leaned in closer to listen, even the man in the window. The Holy Spirit was at His best, and the whole orchestra was playing in fine fashion.

They followed the Scriptures intently, and ultimately, all four men accepted Christ as their personal Lord and Savior.

Our little motley caravan made the trek back to the church, with Biker Babe leading the way. Her head was held high; her steps were resolute; she had seen victories for her Savior.

God uses all sorts of people to do His work: neophytes in their seventies, biker babes, and more—all of whom are soldiers for God. Will you be one of them?

CHAPTER 3

Saint Kitts

§

A COUPLE OF LOCALS FROM Antioch Baptist Church met our group at the Saint Kitts airport, providing a sweet sense of peace and calmness while we endured the mania of customs and seeking out our luggage.

There were eleven team members from various areas: Barbados, Dominica, Trinidad, and several areas in the States. For many, this was their first trip.

The following morning, I sat on my porch, delighted with the Master Architect's manifest beauty. This provided me with a perfect atmosphere to reflect on the mission ahead and to praise Him.

In the distance, I could see a ferry on the crystal-clear, blue-green Caribbean Sea looping along the placid waters on the forty-five-minute journey to the isle of Nevis.

Nevis means "Our Lady of the Snow." This refers to a miraculous snowfall that occurred in the warm climate of Rome. The clouds that encircled the Nevis Peak were reminiscent of this Catholic miracle. On most mission trips, I take a portion of a day to tour the area, taking in the sights and sounds that other tourists come to experience. This is beneficial for two reasons. First, it gives me the opportunity to rejuvenate, and second, since I come into the country on a tourist visa, I need to be able to explain my activities if asked by local authorities. But Saint Kitts is predominately a Christian country, so I had no real reason to fear expulsion by those who vehemently opposed Christianity.

On my excursion day, I learned that Saint Kitts and Nevis are two islands within one country. The country is a commonwealth realm, with

Queen Elizabeth II as the head of state. These islands were among the first in the Caribbean to be settled by Europeans.

Christopher Columbus landed here in 1493; Saint Kitts was named after him, the nickname being a common one for Christopher in the seventeenth century. The islands were separate states until the late nineteenth century, when they were forced to unify. This resulted in a strain between the two countries, causing Nevis to feel that their needs were being neglected in favor of Saint Kitts. In 1983, a move to separate Nevis from Saint Kitts failed with one-third of the vote.

I took the ferry across the Caribbean Sea to Nevis. Land masses sprout from the waters at various intervals; some of these islands are inhabited but others are not.

Bernard was my tour guide for the day. We visited the historic home of the famous English Admiral, Lord Nelson. As the legend goes, when Lord Nelson was killed at sea during the Battle of Trafalgar in 1805, the crew attempted to preserve his body in a barrel of rum. After the long voyage to England, when the barrel was finally opened, it was considerably less than full. Apparently, the sailors on the *Victory* had not minded drinking from a barrel that contained a decomposing body.

Bernard also told me that one of our prominent founding fathers, Alexander Hamilton, was born in Nevis.

After finishing the informative tour, I met my other team members at Antioch Baptist Church for the opening rally. The church was elegant and had a floor-plus-balcony seating capacity of 350. Having no air conditioning, there was an abundance of ceiling fans.

The previous year, seven churches had agreed to participate on this mission, but two had dropped out. So, that night we expected five churches and pastors as well as several volunteers. As the name of each church was called out, its pastor and his volunteers stood up. The missionaries assigned to those groups went over to introduce themselves, do some bonding, and lay out plans for the remainder of the week.

Eagerly awaiting my name to be called, looking forward to meeting the church members I would be working with, I was reminded how plans often change on the mission field. Finally, my name was called as was that of the church I'd been assigned. I was the only one who stood up. My church was a no-show. Time to shift gears! The Lord knew best; He was the Master Conductor who had orchestrated this event.

My responsibilities switched to the host church; I was paired up with Pastor Lincoln Connors. Observing the thirty-one-year-old pastor from afar, my initial impression had been that he was quiet, deliberate, and distracted. But, as often is the case, first impressions can be wrong.

Pastor Connors was bright and articulate. He was like an Energizer Bunny constantly in motion, letting no details escape his eagle eye. Little did I know that Divine Providence had showered me with favor with this fine young pastor. As it turned out, Pastor Connors was the bright, shining light for the nationals and a great force behind the mission. In my mind, Pastor Connors went from being like a mouse to being like a rock.

Sunday-morning service started at nine thirty with an animated praise team. A keyboard player pounded out notes, a drummer thumped the beat, a guitarist strummed, and other musicians blew their instruments, all coming together to make a melody of praise for the Lord. Old ladies and young children danced together in front of the pulpit, caught up in the spirit of the music.

I felt as though I was in the midst of an angelic praise session. This was a *real* "coming to church" event; the Holy Spirit was in attendance, and emotions were at a fever pitch.

For a moment, a twinge of doubt struck my heart. Would this laid-back Southern preacher be able to keep these charming people immersed in the Spirit? Then assurance washed over me, and I remembered that it was all in His hands.

As though I was seeing things in slow motion, Pastor Connors rose, stood at the pulpit, and announced me with a kind and complimentary introduction.

The moment for me to preach had come all too soon. Butterflies invaded my stomach. I took my place behind the pulpit, appearing calm and serene, but within I was battling a storm of nerves. I gripped the pulpit tightly; I saw the congregation full of women arrayed in dazzling, multicolored dresses and adorned in their finest jewels, wearing wide-brimmed hats and corsages, and the men wearing their Sunday best. I took a moment to engrave this scene upon my mind.

One last, deep breath…everything was still moving in slow motion. "Let my words be your words, Lord." And off I went, like a horse out of the gate.

The message was entitled, *"Almost,"* based on Acts 26:28, when Agrippa said to Paul, *"Almost* you have persuaded me to be a Christian." The message captured the congregation's full attention. It was hanging on my every word.

Finally, I stood aside and Pastor Connors resumed his post to offer an invitation. I was elated to see how bountiful the Lord's harvest was; sixty people came forward. Unlike Agrippa, they were certain in their conviction to follow Christ. What a thrilling moment to see so many people coming to Christ.

Church and Sunday school concluded at 1:30 p.m. Tired and sweaty, I found that my day was far from its finish line.

About twenty church members and I were treated to lunch at the lovely home of Sam and Jean Condor. The luncheon was held in honor of Lincoln Connors's seventh year as a pastor. Several members gave eloquent snippets about his many accomplishments. Jean performed a memorable and heartfelt song and dance for him. It was evident by her performance that she was someone special and obvious by their home that the Condors were affluent.

I was intrigued to discover that Sam Condor was the deputy prime minister of Saint Kitts, a career politician. He was physically diminutive, but his presence demanded respect from a giant.

While Pastor Connors was surrounded by his admiring church members, I seized the opportunity to ask the deputy prime minister about the history of Saint Kitts as well as the present social and economic conditions of the country. His answers were thoughtful and deliberate. It was clear this was a discussion he had had many times before and one that he had meditated on privately.

He began by explaining that the sugarcane industry had once been a fruitful money crop for hundreds of years, providing for Saint Kitts. Unfortunately, this had come to a crashing halt five years prior (2005) with the advent of sugar-beet farming, and nothing had filled the financial chasm. Families who had worked for generations on sugar plantations were no longer able to depend upon this once-lucrative career. Now, the majority of the country depended upon the tourist trade. "When the world is in a stagnant economic state, Saint Kitts hurts more than most," he said.

I asked, "How do you keep the young and bright if there are no opportunities?"

His response: "We don't. It is a riddle that must be solved in order for us to compete on the world stage."

This man, whose stride was confident and whose handshakes were engulfing, cared very deeply for his people and country.

My thoughts turned to Grenada, where I knew that unemployment was high and whose society was scourged with drugs. Most citizens were dependent on the government. There was no hope and no future there. My prayer was, "God, please spare these gentle people of Saint Kitts."

My escort, James, drove me up to the police academy, the location of one of Antioch Church's outreach center. Antioch provided five outreach Sunday-school classes in different neighborhoods for people who were not able to attend services. Each center had a biblical name, and this one was called Salem which means peace. There were twenty children, aged three to fourteen, and several adults waiting inside for us.

Salem had been in existence for forty-five years, and James had attended it as a boy. He now showed his gratitude for this place of peace by driving children to and from Sunday school.

Old style, the class started with a recitation of the books of the Bible in order, and then each person repeated a memory verse. When they finished, I shared the Gospel with them through the EvangeCube. The EvangeCube is a puzzle-like cube with seven pictures that clearly unfold the Gospel of Jesus.

The first picture shows the separation that sin causes between man and God. The next pictures show Christ's death on the cross, the open tomb, His resurrection, the choice between heaven and hell, and finally, how to become a follower of Christ. I offered an invitation, and six people accepted Jesus as their Lord and Savior. These added souls for God sent my spirit soaring.

Upon closing, I gave an opportunity for questions and answers. The first question came from an obstinate lady sitting in the back of the room. She hollered out, "Why is there so much racial strife in the USA?"

I responded, "Ma'am, I'm here to talk about Jesus, not civil-rights issues."

She persisted in a blatant fashion. She was loud, angry, and accusatory. The enemy was trying to steal the joy from the room, to derail us, and to stir up consternation. But the power within me was greater than the power within the world. The peace that transcends all understanding filled the room and gave me the divine words of wisdom, pouring out the living water of the Holy Spirit and quenching the fire of animosity.

Without hesitation, I responded to the woman's distraction. "Madam, let me point out to you that in the USA, we have a black president. The head of the Republican Party is black, the president of AARP is black, and the richest woman in America is black. Now, let me ask you a question. Could I, as a white person, be elected to public office in your country?"

"No," she answered.

"Today, we are here to recognize the One who knows no color of skin, only the condition of the heart," I said.

In unison, all the other adults shouted, "Amen!" The children sat as still as statues, staring with wide eyes.

God proved that Salem was a place of peace despite the attempts at disharmony. When we are empty vessels, He fills us and uses us.

The next day began with a sky full of puffy, white clouds; a bright, yellow sun; and hot, humid temperatures. The younger team members chirped like birds at daybreak, with plenty on their platter and eager to go. Some of the older team members' batteries had almost run down after long days and late nights. On this day, I was to meet many of the public officials as well as some of the leading businesspeople, so my mojo was working overtime.

The hotel was kind enough to set aside its restaurant for this occasion. A buzz of excitement hovered in the air. I was allowed the privilege to meet the heads of the social-security, overseas-immigration, and public-works departments, as well as others. Generally speaking, it was difficult to distinguish those who held powerful positions from ordinary citizens. Of course, some, like Sam Condor, had a special flair.

I am often asked how I speak to different church denominations, prisons, and upscale events. My message is always the same: I just use different words and descriptions depending on the event. As Paul, the apostle, did in his lifetime, I shape the style and material to fit the listeners.

On this occasion, I challenged the leaders of Saint Kitts to finish strong. I told them of public officials in my own community who had recently been indicted and come under public scrutiny. Some of these men had been in the twilight of their careers, and now their whole life's work had been tarnished.

My message to this elite group of men was about King Hezekiah. In 2 Kings 18:3, the Bible says, "And he [Hezekiah] did that which was right in the sight of the Lord." Hezekiah had started out as a godly king. His overall reign was one of godliness. God had poured out a plethora of blessings upon him, yet in the end, his arrogance caused him to fall.

Hezekiah did not finish well. His days ended with him being completely self-centered, concerned only about his own personal comfort and his own success.

My message to these men was to be steadfast, strong, and assiduous all the way to the end of life—to remain humble and obedient unto God, not letting pride cause their downfall.

The men hung on my every word as though these were the very ones they needed to hear to sustain their lives. I could see that they were engaged and focused. Afterward, Pastor Connors assured me that the message had been profoundly appropriate and very well received.

Following this meeting with the leaders, I visited a lovely lady who divided her time between London and Saint Kitts. She was a lifelong friend of Jean Condor's. Her home was elegant and sat on a hill overlooking the city and the Caribbean Sea. She had a soft, gentle spirit, and her British accent was pleasing to the ear.

After I explained the Gospel to her, she was eager to accept. She had been plagued with a nagging doubt about her salvation.

Romans 10:9 says, "If you declare with your mouth, 'Jesus is Lord,' and believe in your heart that God raised Him from the dead, you will be saved."

John 10:28–29 says, "I give them eternal life, and they shall never perish; no one can snatch them out of My hand. My Father, who has given them to Me, is greater than all; no one can snatch them out of My Father's hand."

These verses resonated truth within her soul and provided her with full assurance. She prayed the sinner's prayer and gained renewed confidence that her salvation was secure.

The following morning, the mission team gathered around the pool for a time of prayer. Some team members were going to a public school to share the Gospel. I, however, had the early hours of the day set aside for sermon preparation, and I was looking forward to a quiet morning of study and reflection. I soon discovered that the Maestro had other plans for me.

One of the team members had developed debilitating stomach cramps and a fever. She was unable to go to the school, leaving a position that needed filling. I abandoned my quiet morning to fill the gap and go to the school.

The school was old, with an unappealing, dusty playground. It was a two-story, gray cement structure. The open, louvered windows allowed the noises of other classes to float in and out like the breeze from the sea.

As we entered the building, the bell rang, and the children meandered to their classes like water in a swiftly flowing river. The children were loud, boisterous, giddy, pompous, and proud, just like most other schoolchildren. They all wore uniforms much like the ones our parochial schoolchildren wear.

I stood before twenty sixth-grade students sitting at perfectly aligned desks. These children were the same age as my grandchildren, Hannah and Caleb. (Though worlds apart, both sets of children are curious little wiggle worms.) Their eyes seemed to wonder, "What is this white guy going to say?"

I presented the EvangeCube to them. With each turn of the cube, the students grew more still and more focused. At the conclusion, fifteen children raised their hands to pray the sinner's prayer. What a tremendous victory for the Lord.

Before I left, the students treated me with the gift of their school song, which they sang with great pride and gusto.

I praised God, thanking Him for rearranging my agenda for the day. What an honor and a treat to speak to these young people, to witness their hearts change for Him.

I pondered upon how much Saint Kitts's present-day schools are like those I attended in the 1940s and 1950s. Saint Kitts still taught right from wrong, moral values, and Christian concepts. But in 1960s America, these views became suspect in the eyes of a very liberal government. As far as the school systems, I think that Christian values resonate more in Saint Kitts than with our own government policies.

My next visit was with Devon, who was a pleasant man around forty years old with an engaging smile. As I chatted with him, I discovered that I was sitting in the presence of a local celebrity. Devon was also known as Lord Kut, the premiere Calypso singer of Saint Kitts. This explained his colorful, vibrant, and animated attire.

He knew that people had been praying for him, believers who were concerned about his salvation and his heart. He listened to me present the Gospel to him. He was pliable like clay in the Potter's hand, sensitive to the leading of the Holy Spirit. He drank the truth in. He accepted it as eagerly as a desert pilgrim accepts water.

I encouraged him to use his God-given talent for the Lord. This was a novel idea for Lord Kut, but I could see in his furrowed brow that his creative mind was already in motion. A seed was planted; now may a harvest be produced.

Nightfall approached, and I made my way back to the hotel. As I lay my head on my pillow and closed my eyes, I reflected on the day's activities. I had had a well-planned agenda for the day, but God's plans had prevailed.

What pure joy it was to be in the Lord's work. My heart soared with gratitude that He had chosen me and given me the privilege to serve Him in so many diverse places, to a variety of unique people.

My prayer was that I would accept the challenges ahead of me with peace; that I would be emboldened with inspiration to fulfill His great commission.

The next day, my driver was a delightful, jovial nurse named Mary. Even though she had worked a full eight-hour shift the night before, she greeted me with an attitude of cheerfulness, enthusiasm, and readiness.

She ushered me to the appropriate neighborhood. As I went and spoke with neighbors, she remained steadfastly by my side, quietly cheering the listeners on to receive His truth through prayer. We began walking to our next appointment when this mighty prayer warrior saw a fellow nurse sitting on her front porch. The two ladies exchanged pleasantries. It was apparent that there was a close bond between them.

However, the nurse friend was the complete opposite of joyous Mary. She was twice Mary's age, cranky, and not the least bit hospitable to me. It was obvious she was happy to see Mary but wanted nothing to do with this white preacher guy.

The customary, polite thing to do in the Caribbean when someone greets you on the porch is to invite him or her in and offer some form of hospitality. The nurse friend was having none of this. Instead, she remained staunchly fixed on her porch, eating out of a bowl of chips and drinking iced tea. Even though it was mid-morning, the sun was hot, causing us to sweat profusely.

Despite the friend's animosity toward me, I began sharing the Gospel with her. She, in turn, crunched her chips as obnoxiously as possible and rattled her ice cubes against the glass with every swig. She acted as though she was not listening to me and could not care less about what I was saying.

Occasionally, she looked over at Mary and made a snide remark about what I was saying, hoping to derail the witness. I was suited in the full armor of God; slingshots, arrows, and sullenness could not distract me from the mission at hand.

As I continued to speak and warrior Mary continued to quietly pray, the nurse's veil of disinterest slowly began to come off as the Word of God penetrated her heart. Her countenance softened, she sat quietly, and her heart opened up as the truth spread into her conscience like a wildfire. She accepted Christ as her Lord and Savior.

Now, Mary not only had a friend, but also a new sister in Christ.

Still praising God for His sweet, gentle Spirit and the amazing transformation He made in the nurse's life, my mind switched gears to consider my next appointment at Her Majesty's Prison. If God can make pliable a hardened nurse's heart, what incredible work will He do in the hearts of contemptuous convicts?

Six of us, three women and three men, traveled downtown to witness the love and grace of Jesus Christ to the inmates. The prison still carried the name Her Majesty's Prison, a throwback to the colonial days. The structure was old and haggard from many years of use.

While standing at the prison entrance, waiting to be scrutinized by those in charge, I noticed the count board. HMP contained 250 men and three women. After we were appropriately inspected by the authorities, we were led into a large, open space inside the main prison, the area where the men's showers were.

A female guard escorted our three mission ladies over to the women inmates. These sweet servants had never set foot inside a prison before; I watched as they anxiously went away toward the unknown. Though they were uncertain of the events that were to occur beyond those steel doors with massive locks, they were confident in the One who had brought them there.

My group of men then passed through two armored doors, entering into a large, dank, cinder-block room with cells on the perimeter. Most of the inmates were on their best behavior, sitting in uneven rows of folding metal chairs. The unruly ones were in cells. Occasionally, I could see faces with black eyes of twisted torment peering out from the darkness, hands squeezing the life out of the bars. It was hot and humid in this dungeon-like facility. Body odors were pungent, and sweat moved down faces like running water.

One of our team members started things off by playing his guitar and singing songs. This lightened the mood considerably and loosened everyone up. The inmates were delighted to be entertained. They clapped along with the beat of the music, even cheering with excitement.

When the music ended, Pastor Connors introduced me as a man who had once himself been a prisoner, now turned preacher. This immediately gave me credibility; all eyes were riveted on me.

I told the inmates that Jesus Christ had sent me specifically to this prison to share with them the hope and love He had to offer them. "One day, you will stand before the Judge of judges; He will ask you only one question: did you accept my Son, Jesus Christ, as your Savior, or did you reject Him? Your last appointment before a judge did not go so well. Today is the day to know the answer to the Judge's question. The answer will determine where you spend eternity."

Several of these men were convicted by the Spirit and raised their hands to be set free and to live out their lives with Jesus as their Savior. These men might not have been free physically, but they were free spiritually and for all of eternity.

The guards allowed an older inmate to come speak with me. He shared that he was sixty-five years old and believed that God was giving him this last opportunity to make things right by surrendering his life to Christ. He willingly and joyfully accepted Christ as his Savior.

When we met back with our three ladies, their looks of uncertainty and anxiety had washed away, replaced with those of exaltation and praise.

They radiated such joy that they could have brought light into the darkest room. With great excitement, they told us that all three female inmates had accepted Jesus as their Savior. More precious names had been entered into the Lamb's Book of Life.

The sermon for the closing night was titled "Hosea and the Whore." This is an incredible story that pictures our Redeemer who loves us even though we wander from Him and go toward sin.

Hosea, a faithful prophet, obeyed the command of God to marry Gomer, a prostitute. When Gomer left the marriage and returned to her old lifestyle, Hosea showed mercy to her by finding her, forgiving her, and bringing her back home. This is an astonishing story of our merciful God's love and forgiveness for all sinners who place their faith in Jesus Christ.

I closed with the statement, "The Son, the Son: who will take the Son?" Other than my voice, the only sound that could be heard was the soft hum of the ceiling fans. The Holy Spirit was present among us and penetrating each and every heart. It was a sweet, holy, and emotional dedication in which all the glory, praise, and honor went unto the Almighty. People poured down to the altar to make their decisions public.

God had triumphed over evil. He certainly visited the island of Saint Kitts and claimed hundreds for His very own. I could almost hear the musical instruments of the heavenly choir, all in tune, playing the hallelujah chorus, celebrating the new recruits for God's army.

I hid myself behind the cross and gave God all the glory. I praised God for allowing me to be a participant.

Ecclesiastes 12:13 reads, "Let us hear the conclusion of the whole matter: Fear God and keep His commandments, for this is the whole duty of man."

Billy Gray and Pastor Connors

Our Lady of Snow

Congregation wearing their Sunday best

Nurse Mary and her friend

CHAPTER 4

Barbados

§

BARBADOS IS A CARIBBEAN ISLAND bestowed with beauty. The country is small, with a population of 285,000 and an area of twenty-one by fourteen miles.

It is the birthplace of the famous singer Rihanna and the setting of the second homes of well-known people like Oprah Winfrey and Tiger Woods. The west side of the island has rambling homes and plush yards situated among expansive resorts and spas for the wealthy to vacation and relax in.

The southwestern side is more of a touristy area for the less afflu-ent, with white beaches and the calm Caribbean Sea. The east side has huge Atlantic Ocean waves pleasing to avid surfers. The area is lined with mountains and rugged cliffs, its rocky beaches dotted with bungalows. The northern side is a plateau area with 491 sprawling sugarcane farms.

It takes about two hours to drive the perimeter of the island. The roads are very narrow and curvy, and traffic is slow; otherwise, the trip could be made in about an hour.

Although I have been to many Caribbean Islands, this was a real treat for me, because Trista, my daughter, came along. This was her first mis-sion trip, and I was a proud Poppa. There is something special and inscru-table about a first trip. I could see that Trista was nervous and had high expectations. I wondered if she was up to the task. I could sense some inner turmoil within her, although not a word was spoken about it.

Tropical Storm Betty caused us long delays as we waited in the Miami airport, which did nothing to calm our nerves. But twenty-four hours af-ter leaving home, we arrived at our hotel, finding it to be very nice. French doors opened onto our balcony with a view of the beach and the Caribbean Sea across the street.

The real proof of a successful mission trip is how well the nationals have prepared for us and how dedicated the local leaders are. At orientation on our first day, we met Hal, his wife Cheryl, and our team leader, Rudy. They were committed. We were off to a good start.

The three other members of our team were Marge Pratt, a member of the Destin United Methodist Church; Dr. Carla Hinds; and her son, Andrew; they were from First Baptist Church of Destin and also both first timers.

On Sunday morning, I preached a sermon on the rich man and the poor man, the parable found in Luke 16:20–25. Four professions of faith were made. After a vivacious and charismatic round of songs, we broke off into Sunday-school groups.

Afterward, the church provided us with a buffet-style lunch consisting of flying fish, jerked chicken, baked macaroni, and salad. (This was consistently our meal). Over lunch, we had the opportunity to get better acquainted with Hal, Cheryl, and Rudy.

Hal was a national champion—a karate hall of famer, the Chuck Norris of Barbados. He was the pastor at the Community Christian Fellowship Church to which we had been assigned. The building also doubled as a gym where he instructed in karate. He loved the Lord and had a heart for youth.

Cheryl was a phenomenal teacher to the teenage girls. She spoke slowly and from the heart, often with her eyes closed. She knew the Word of God inside and out. She taught the girls how to read their Bible daily, how to take notes, and how to highlight important passages in their Bibles. She wanted the girls to dig deep and to thirst after the Word.

Rudy was a kind man with a constant, radiant smile on his face. He sang loud and proud, looking straight up to the Lord with his hands raised as though he could see the King upon His throne. His love for the Lord was obvious. He worked in construction, but he desired to be a pastor.

All three of these saints of God proved to be bold witnesses and extremely beneficial in getting people to open their doors to us within the downtrodden neighborhoods where we witnessed.

One day, we were invited to speak at a school for delinquent boys. This rowdy, rambunctious group of a thousand students came into a large auditorium with no seats. Hal gave an incredible karate performance, which commanded respect and ensured the attention and good behavior of this motley crew.

Yes, in the Barbados schools, we were allowed to preach the Gospel of Jesus Christ and to give an altar call. How about that!

I then gave my testimony. I shared with everyone that I had accepted Christ at the age of eight. "My Christian growth was slow during the first part of my life, and after college, I entered into the practice of law. Success came both socially and financially. My devotion and focus was on money and materialism.

"My life came to a shattering halt when I was charged with conspiracy and imprisoned for nine years. While in prison, I began searching for the Lord.

"I carried a nagging doubt about the decision that I had made as a youth. So, I publicly confessed that I was a sinner and wanted Christ as my Lord. I've been sharing His story to prisoners, students, villages, tribes, and churches all over the world ever since. Now I am devoted to God, and He is my primary focus."

I encouraged these boys to surrender their hearts and lives to Christ, to trust and obey Him. "Life is hard whether we choose Christ or not, but with God, we have a Father Who will never forsake us and Who loves us just as we are."

At the conclusion, 119 boys professed their faith in Jesus Christ. It was amazing, seeing these hard, calloused boys transform into pliable material for the Lord to shape and mold for His purpose.

Another day, Rudy and I were canvassing a down-and-out neighborhood. It was hot, humid, and still. Many in this area had no electricity. Some sat on their porches, fanning themselves with funeral-home fans.

We came to a house, larger than most, with no front door and several broken windows. We hollered out, "Hello! Anyone home?" as was our custom.

A tall, muscular man walked out. "What's you got?" he asked.

I responded, "Did you know, I came all the way from the United States just to see you?"

"Me?"

"Yes, you."

He sat down on the front steps and invited me to join him.

I asked, "Are you an athlete?"

He responded, "Man, how did you know?"

"Well, you walk like one and have the body for it. Tell me your story."

He told me he was called JL. "I was raised here, in Barbados," he said. "Seven children in all. We were poor. One day at school, a man introduced us to the game of basketball. We had seen some on TV, but most of us played soccer. It seemed as though I had a natural talent for basketball. I got bigger and bigger and better and better. Soon, the school and the community started giving me special privileges. People knew me wherever I went. Then I made our Olympic team.

"I met a white girl from New York. She liked the fame and recognition. We got married, and before we knew it, we had three little girls.

"But my fame began to fade like yesterday's newspaper. Job opportunities dried up almost overnight, as I was not really qualified to do nothing.

"My wife came from an affluent family. After her mother came to see us and saw that her daughter was not living in the style she was accustomed to, she took her daughter and the three little girls back to New York. One day, I came home from work, and they were gone. And I ain't seen them in three years. I'm a broken man, Mister Billy. Just don't care anymore."

I asked him, "JL, have you ever heard of Jesus?"

"Yes, when I was a boy. But ain't he dead now?"

"No, JL, Jesus is alive, right here, and is living in my heart as we speak."

I then explained the Gospel to him in a rudimentary fashion.

JL began to weep as he heard that Jesus had died for him, paid a price he could not pay, and would love and care for him even if the whole world rejected him.

We prayed the sinner's prayer; he wept for joy.

Rudy, who had been standing in the street, came forward and was instructed to mentor this giant of a man, to love on him, and to teach him.

This was a delightful mission trip, one that I will always cherish. The gift of seeing my daughter propagating the Gospel of Jesus Christ was priceless; it does not get any better than that.

Now, you'll hear Trista's story of the trip and her insight on her first mission.

§

After twenty-four hours of travel, delayed by Tropical Storm Betty, we finally arrived at our hotel. Poppa and I shared a room with two full-size beds.

The next morning, I stepped out onto the balcony to have my quiet time, and I was delighted to have a view of the Caribbean Sea. What a treat! I could see the turquoise-blue sea and the white beach.

As I sat on the balcony, a little Barbados bullfinch bird flew over and sat on the arm of my chair. She continued to sit there as I had my quiet time. It was as though God had sent me a little friend who was intent on seeing what I was doing. All her other bullfinch friends were flying around, searching for food here and there.

I named her Tricie, after my beloved grandmother. Since she seemed so interested in me, I confided to her that I was nervous about witnessing and that I missed my family.

Up to this point in my married life, I had been a stay-at-home mom for nearly ten years, which had given me the opportunity to attend all of my children's events. The Lord had graciously permitted me to be a part of Hannah's and Caleb's daily lives. However, while I was on my trip, the children were in Vacation Bible School, something I had been a part of for many years. Hannah was the lead actress in a long skit she would perform in front of the entire VBS audience of several hundred people, and my heart ached that I could not be there to witness this milestone in her life.

However, my sweet and faithful husband, Mike, had stepped in for me. He spent the week working his full-time job, taking care of the children, and serving at VBS.

Betsey, Mike's mother, also worked at VBS and took care of Hannah and Caleb while Mike was at work. So I knew that the children were in capable hands. But still…Little Tricie listened to all my woes.

My mind shifted back to the Lord. I experienced a peace and a calm that was unexplainable. I thanked Him for sending me this feathered friend. I chuckled at His sense of humor, because I only like birds at a distance. But Tricie was different. She had been sent by God to comfort me, which she faithfully did each morning that I spent with the Lord on that balcony in Barbados.

The roads in Barbados are narrow and curvy, barely wide enough to fit two cars side by side. Bajans drive on the left side of the road in a fast and manic way, as though they are angry, even though they are not. They constantly honk their horns and wave and smile at one another. The island is so small that it seems as though everyone knows the other. Every few yards, there is a roundabout. Driving there is a dizzy and woozy ride.

Bajans speak English but have heavy Caribbean accents, so to me, it often sounded as though they were speaking a different language. The people are beautiful in a natural and free-spirited way. They are very colorful. The women are strong and robust, with large muscles in their arms and legs. They have big smiles and radiate with joy.

Our first visit was to Cheryl's house, where we had an appointment with her daughter's friend, Shakiyah. Cheryl informed us that Kimberly, her daughter, and Shakiyah were both fifteen years old and had been lifelong friends.

Shakiyah had been raised in the church and was saved several years ago, but her walk with Christ had come to a halt, and her faith was wavering. At the age of twelve, she had begun hanging out with the wrong crowd, getting involved with boys, drinking, and marijuana. Her concerned mother had asked her pastor to counsel Shakiyah.

Well, this wolf dressed in sheep's clothing secretly made promises and advances to this young girl, all of which she allowed because she trusted the adult pastor. At the tender age of thirteen, she had found herself in love with this man and pregnant. The scandal was made public.

The man resigned, moved with his wife and other children to a neighboring island, and had nothing to do with Shakiyah or their nearly two-year-old daughter.

Shakiyah was left with a child to raise, a broken heart, and a shattered faith. Cheryl and Kimberly loved on Shakiyah and her daughter and tried to win her back to Christ, but her hurt was too deep.

We drove into this modest Bajan neighborhood that had dirt roads, houses scattered about, and a local neighborhood liquor store. Alcoholism and marijuana abuse was a major affliction there, along with infidelity and fornication. The nicer homes were made of cinder blocks; other homes were made of scrap metal and patches of wood. Chickens and roosters roamed the streets, along with cats and dogs.

Four of us team members sat in a small room with Cheryl, Kimberly, Shakiyah, Shakiyah's daughter, and another small child. Both the little ones bounced from lap to lap the entire visit.

The home was of cinder block, with round arches. It had small rooms, no air conditioning, and raised windows; the front door was opened to allow a breeze to flow through. We introduced ourselves and had some small talk.

Then Poppa said, "Trista, you share with Shakiyah your testimony." Nothing like being put on the spot to bring you right out of your shell. With fear, trembling, and trepidation, I did as I was asked.

I shared my story with this fifteen-year-old unwed mother. "At the age of eight, I began following Jesus Christ. But as a teenager, I took my eyes off Christ and set my focus on things of the world. I chased after every party, living a life of pleasure and recklessness. I sought happiness in people, parties, and living a self-serving lifestyle.

"As a young adult, I found myself lonely and unhappy. The partying lifestyle no longer pleased me, and the people around me caused me great pain. My life was going away from God; my only hope was to go back toward Him.

"As a child, I had admitted I was a sinner, believed Jesus died for me to save me from my sins, and confessed that He was my Lord and Savior. As a young adult, I was still saved despite my sinful lifestyle, but I had strayed from God's path and His plan for me. I had to admit to God that I was living a sinful lifestyle and ask Him to help me get back onto His path, leaving the old path behind. I had to believe I was still God's child, loved, and forgiven by Him. And I had to commit to live for Him, not for the next party.

"Shakiyah, God still loves you too, and He is waiting with open arms for you to come back to Him. You can trust Him. He will never hurt you or leave you."

With tears in her eyes, Shakiyah said, "I'm ready to live for Him and not no dumb, lyin', cheatin' man."

After praying with Shakiyah, we walked the dirt roads, going from house to house, witnessing to people. We even witnessed inside the liquor store, a convenience store, and a barber shop.

The following day, we talked with some men hanging out in the street. I spoke to Jerry, a longtime friend of Rudy's, who said he knew Jesus and that he prayed to God but had never asked Jesus into his heart. We talked a very long time. He listened and conversed with me, but he never would commit to the Lord. I felt as though I had fallen short.

The next morning, my little friend Tricie and I sat on the porch and watched the sunrise over the Caribbean Sea. I was reflecting over the events of the day before and telling God and Tricie how ineffective and inadequate I felt. Then God pointed me to several verses.

Philippians 3:9 showed me that I was to be found in Christ, to be as one with Him—having faith in Christ and not in my own efforts. The goal was not for me to win the battle through my own effectiveness; rather, the goal was for me to win Christ by being found in Him. I was to win Him by being so intertwined with Him that I went wherever He went.

He is the Victor always leading us to victory (2 Corinthians 2:14).

God gives strength to those who wait on Him; it is His strength and power where the efficacy and the success comes from (Isaiah 40:31). It was not my job to change people's beliefs. My job was to cling to Him like a little girl clings onto her daddy's neck.

My mind drifted back to when I was a little girl around five years old. My family and I were at the beach in Destin. Poppa loved going out on the raft and riding the waves; he wanted me to go with him. I did not like the waves, because they scared me. I liked the calm water.

Poppa promised to take care of me and not to let anything hurt me. Well, if Poppa said I would be safe, then there was no doubt that I would be safe. Why? Because I trusted him completely. So, he put me on the float, lying on my stomach. He held on to one of my arms while his other arm was wrapped around me, holding on to the raft. The waves were huge. Water was splashing in my face, Poppa was laughing, and I was trusting fully in him to protect me.

Suddenly, a huge wave came crashing down on top of us with full force. I flew off the raft, the raft flew up into the air, and Poppa got swept off his feet.

The next thing I remember, I was sitting on the sandy floor underneath the water. I looked to my left; I could see the very scary deep, dark green Gulf, where all the sharks and other scary sea monsters lived. I looked to my right; I could see waves crashing toward the beach. I looked forward; I could see Poppa's feet.

I did not even try to get to the surface. I just sat there, holding my breath, waiting on Poppa to pull me up. He said he would take care of me, and I trusted him to do so.

As I was focused on Poppa, I saw his hand reach down. He pulled me out of the water. I clung onto his neck so tightly that not even a tidal wave could have broken my grip. I knew that his strength would get me back to the beach and that my job was to hold on to him tightly.

I realized that my purpose on this trip was to bind myself to the Lord, obediently going wherever He went and trusting Him to do the work of soul saving, just like I had trusted Poppa to get me back to the beach.

That afternoon, we stopped at a park with lots of men hanging out and smoking pot while small children played on the playground unattended. I spoke to Jim, a tall, slender man with long dreadlocks and a cap with a marijuana leaf proudly displayed on his forehead. Reggae music was blaring, and the men continued smoking their weed. Jim and I talked extensively. He told me he knew of Jesus, but he was not saved. "You don't know all the mess I've been in. I've done a lotta sinnin'. I'm one bad dude. Not too many folks want nothin' to do with me, 'cause I'm always gettin' into trouble."

I asked, "Jim, do you have a girlfriend or a wife?"

"Yeah, I gotta girlfriend." He told me about her and how much he loved her.

I asked, "How do you show your love for her?"

He said, "I spend time with her. I talk to her nice, listen to her, and buy her stuff."

I said, "Well, God wants to spend time with you too. He loves you more than you love your girlfriend. He wants you to confess your sins to Him so He can forgive you and save you from hell. God will be your Lord and Savior if you ask and believe."

Teary eyed, Jim said, "You mean, God will forgive every sin there is?"

He was overwhelmed that God would forgive him for all of his sins and that God actually wanted to spend time with him for all of eternity. He prayed the sinner's prayer, asking Jesus to be His Savior.

I later found out from Rudy that Jim had just gotten out of jail for murdering someone, somehow convincing another man to take the blame for him. It was probably a good thing I had not known that up front. Only an awesome God can use a little white girl to lead a pot-smoking murderer to Christ. He loves us all and is willing to save us all.

This trip forced me out of the comfort zone of my home and placed me in a foreign country, fully dependent upon Him. It challenged me to allow others to help me at home so I could serve Him in a new way. Though I had missed a special event in Hannah's life, God had provided her with all the support she needed, and I got to see the play on video.

This trip showed me the importance of clinging to the Lord and relying on His words and His strength. I saw some people saved, and I witnessed some people refuse. But God does not send us on a mission to coerce people to believe in Him; He sends us to plant the seeds. We are then to allow Him to do the watering and the growing.

When I was trembling and shaking, He was my strength. When I felt hopeless and disheartened, He was my hope. This trip was all about Him and His power; I was just a small tool that He used.

God can use anyone on the mission field. If He can use this painfully shy homebody who deals with various maladies, He can use you too. If He calls you, *go*! You will never regret saying yes!

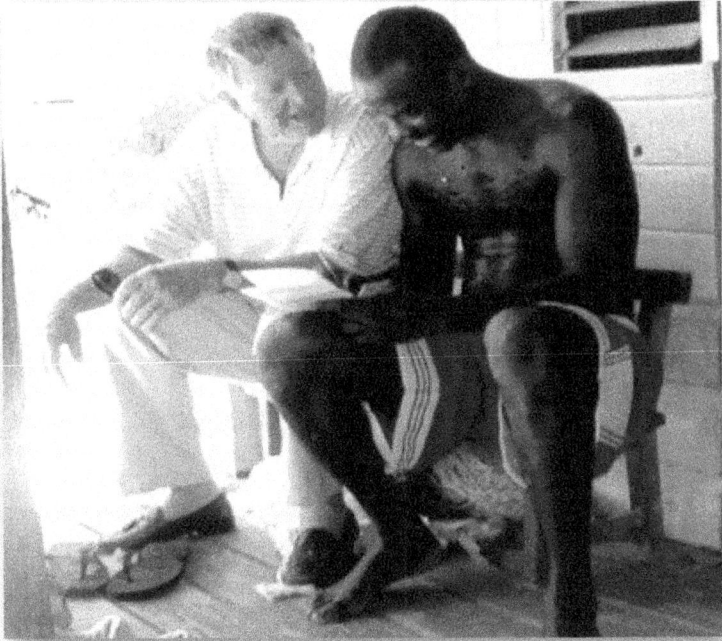

Billy sharing the Gospel with JL, the athlete

Billy and Trista

CHAPTER 5

France

§

I RECEIVED A CALL FROM my longtime friend, Steve. "Hey, you want to go to France in two weeks?"

Steve, the vice president of international commission, was in charge of India and surrounding areas. "What's in France?" I asked.

"Well, they have enough workers, but they need more preachers," he said in his middle-Tennessee accent.

I was certainly intrigued, but many things would have to fall into place in a hurry. Would I need a visa? Would I need shots? Could I raise enough money for the trip in such a short time? However, the main question was—was it God's will for me to go? My fleece (test) was, if God raised the money, I would go.

I mailed a letter to my supporters, and within ten days, I had secured sufficient funds. So, my journey began. The flight from Atlanta to France took eight-and-a-half hours. France is nine hours ahead of Central Time.

As the 747 was making its descent into the Charles de Gaulle International Airport, a surge of excitement rippled through my body. This was my first visit here. Since I was traveling alone, I hoped the stranger assigned to pick me up from the airport would be there.

There I was, among hordes of bustling people speaking a language I did not understand, following signs I could not read. My heart was beating faster than it did during a thirty-minute jog on a treadmill. Once through customs, I saw the most beautiful sign: "Welcome Billy Gray," held by a man named David. My fear was replaced with alacrity.

I was given a private and interesting tour of Paris by Alan Whitely and Janet Claxton. I was to go to Limoges, a three-hour train ride south of Paris—a plum assignment.

The train ride was delightful. I used the time to sit back, relax, and enjoy God's glorious creation.

The train, which traveled a hundred miles per hour, stopped every thirty minutes in small hamlets, each of which had its own décor and personality. The countryside was gorgeous, with rolling hills and fields full of cattle and horses.

Limoges is known worldwide for its porcelain products. Its population is approximately two hundred thousand. It is a university town and a little more liberal than the average French town. Some of the brightest minds of France and Africa reside there. The French had brought in the brightest Africans to do research and to train in computer science and math. Many came from Senegal, a French-speaking Muslim country in Western Africa.

My accommodations were to be in a private residence. I was not looking forward to that, but God soon expunged my fears. My hosts were Alain and Manou DuFour and their twenty-three-year-old daughter, Ludimilla. They were a charming, upper-middle-class family. Alain was a financial planner, and Manou helped in his business, but their main focus was on serving the Lord.

Alain's English was minimal and Manou's was just a bit better, while Ludimilla's was excellent. She was my interpreter when I preached. Girls raised in Christian homes are a small minority among the French.

The DuFour's had a lovely home in the countryside; I had my own private quarters. The rolling hills there reminded me of Tennessee.

It took me two days to understand the family's eating patterns. I had to learn to pace myself while eating the delicious, large meals. Each one began with soup or an appetizer and then went on to a large entrée, followed by a salad with cheese and bread, and then topped off with a dessert. It would have been considered offensive not to eat all the food.

The hospitality of the DuFour's proved to be outstanding during the entire trip; the meals were excellent, and my privacy was never threatened.

As I looked out of the window across the bucolic view from my room, it was difficult to visualize this land being trampled on by hard-booted Germans in World War II. But what was even harder to think about was all the young American soldiers who had given their lives on the beach of Normandy, just north of where I sat.

The next day, we were in two separate meetings that ran on until 10:00 p.m. Their purpose was to give instructions and to rally our spirits. But the air in the balloon had long been deflated before the conclusion of the matter. It was like a scrimmage before game day. The players, exasperated from it, do not come to the game with fresh legs or soaring spirits.

There were five of us on this mission: Mary Lester of Aurora, Colorado; Martha Cesario, from Grand Junction, Colorado; John Kelly of Bienne, Texas, Melody Aslin, from Roseville, Colorado; and me.

I had served with Mary and Martha previously in India and Africa. Both of these ladies were in their early seventies.

John was a superintendent of his school district. This was his first mission trip. He was a man in his midforties with graying hair and a soft voice; he was highly intelligent. He had seven children; six were boys.

We worked with the Église (Church) Évangélique Baptiste. It was known as the little church with a big ear. This church was an anomaly, having only sixty-four members but with sixteen nationalities represented. Of the congregation, 50 percent was African, 25 percent was Caucasian, and 25 percent was Asian.

We started the day with prayer, praise, and singing. Then we were given a mini tour of Limoges. We visited the courthouse, where we were well received and given a special tour.

Our group walked over to the Musée (museum) Municipal de l'Évêché located next the Cathédrale Saint-Étienne de Limoges. We saw artifacts, sculptures, and paintings. The artists' pictures of Christ were beautiful, yet they reminded me of heathens singing Christian songs. The ancient artists painted the Creator of life with no understanding of Who He was.

The following day's services lasted an enjoyable three hours, with lots of African-style praise and worship music, dancing, and hand waving. Though few in number, these believers were fervent; they offered a sweet redolence of harmony. They were bent more toward the Pentecostal way of worshipping rather than the Baptist way. I saw no other Protestant churches in Limoges, but I am sure there were more.

Pastor Luc Masse's oratory style was evangelistic. He was a diminutive, fiery preacher who was full of zeal.

At our opening rally the previous night, there had only been a handful of French pastors. This was not encouraging, causing me to be skeptical of the preparations. The organizers told us to not expect a great harvest, because the Western European mindset was so closed to Christianity. Many were agnostic, believing in no god. Unlike Asia, Africa, or South America, the French were not seeking the truth.

Upon hearing this, I thought, *We are not accountants. That one person who claims Christ as his Lord and Savior may be the next Apostle Paul or Billy Graham. One person could change the destiny of France, of Western Europe, or even of the world. After all, this is the Lord's battle, not ours.*

As the day moved on, it became more apparent that our church had done very little preparation. Pastor Luc had a conference to attend the following day. Much prayer was needed to make our visit a success.

Basil, the assistant pastor, took over the leadership. He proved to be very capable of the challenge and soon became a close confidant. Typically, the host church arranges appointments to visit unsaved people, but we were told that no appointments had been scheduled.

A cloud of disappointment hung over our heads like in a Charlie Brown cartoon. Those of us who were veterans knew this meant door-to-door witnessing and cold calling. This is a challenge even for the most seasoned missionary. Tenacity did not loom large in the novices, and fear resonated in the unknown.

I huddled with our team members. I told them, "This is not going to be an easy mission. Our approach will be far different from that in Asia or Africa—it will be, 'Come, let us reason together,' and not so much of an emotional experience. The French will be hard to reach. Remember, 'It is impossible to please God without faith.' Let us take Romans 8:28 and brand it on our hearts and minds." The pep talk worked temporarily.

The next morning, I had breakfast with the DuFour's. We had a delightful drive into the city where the church was. The winds were high, and the weather was cold.

As the team arrived with a few volunteers, we sang and prayed in the cold little church. At last, it was time to go into the battlefield, where spiritual warfare would take place.

On that chilly afternoon, I saw a young couple snuggled up on a park bench. Approaching them, I asked if they would like to hear the greatest love story ever told. They both spoke English, and the young man, who was a student, looked at his girlfriend, and in a voice of superiority, he said, "Give it your best shot, old man."

I handed both of them a tract and started a dialogue, when he suddenly interrupted me and asked, "Have you ever seen Jesus?"

"No," I answered.

"Then how can you believe in someone you have never seen?" He looked at his girlfriend and winked as if he had gotten me.

I said, "May I ask you a question?"

"Sure, old man," he sneered.

I asked, "Do you believe in Napoleon?"

"Of course," he replied. "He was a great historical figure."

I asked, "Do you believe he was once a ruler of France?"

He responded, "Everybody knows that."

I asked, "Have you ever seen Napoleon?"

I could see the air coming out of the obtuse young man, who said, "No."

"Then how can you believe in Napoleon when you've never seen him?" I asked.

"Well, history tells us about Napoleon," he answered.

I asked, "Did you know there are a thousand times more historical facts written about Jesus than there are about Napoleon?"

His dogmatism had been defeated. He was embarrassed. The two excused themselves and made a hasty retreat.

We spent much of our time witnessing at Champ de Juillet, a park where prostitutes worked for a living flaunting their wares. It was not terribly cold, but the winds blew at a brisk pace, making it bone chilling and very uncomfortable. Seeds were sown, but there was no harvest.

Older people seemed almost obstinate about the Gospel. Many, old and young believed in no god. The smirk on people's faces made me want to recoil and snap back. It was only through the power of the Holy Spirit that I refrained.

While on this trip, President Bush ordered all Americans out of Israel. March 19, 2003, the United States went to war with Iraq. Some of our team members were rebuked for being Americans, but mostly for propagating the Gospel.

The people and government of France, in general, had negative thoughts about the war and Americans. The French looked at Americans as socially and intellectually a step below them.

I summoned the team for another pep talk, reminding them that people were not rejecting the messengers but His Message.

One day, we witnessed in the marketplace. People were happy and relaxed. Some walked, some biked, and some drove cars that looked like tin cans on wheels.

Muslims and anti-Americans were prevalent. The people wanted to know why Americans wanted to kill innocent women and children.

My response was, "We are not here to publicly debate political issues but to share the eternal truth that Jesus Christ is Lord."

The rest of our day was spent in the park, where the benches were filled with older Muslim men. They happily engaged me in conversation. Our talks generally followed the same pattern. "Yes, we know all about Jesus. One of the finest men who ever lived, a great prophet, a great teacher, but not the Son of God. Oh, we worship the same god. He just has a different name," they would say.

Some knew Scripture, but none knew the Lord that saves.

At the end of the day, one woman received Christ, and another young man expressed some interest.

Our final full day approached; a beautiful morning. The sun was warm and radiant. Horses plodded along in the plush, green grass. Spring was as evident as puberty in a boys' locker room.

My sermon subject was Hosea and Gomer, the whore. There is always laughing, groaning, and shock when prostitutes are mentioned, but this audience listened very quietly; the Holy Spirit was present.

Only the God of Heaven could write such a beautiful and compassionate love story. Only God could reach down from heaven and show such amazing love, mercy, and forgiveness to a harlot who wanted nothing to do with Him.

God continually showed Gomer love, forgiveness, and mercy, even when she was unfaithful to Him and to Hosea. It was only by God's divine love that Hosea lovingly brought Gomer home, cleaned her up, and transformed her into a beautiful bride again.

This consistent love, forgiveness, and mercy changed Gomer's heart. The people in Limoges also needed this consistent love, forgiveness, and mercy shown to them.

At the conclusion of my sermon, the majority of the congregation came down to the altar, vowing to continue witnessing to the city that was flooded with unyielding hearts.

At the closing rally, I told the congregation that the United Nations could learn from its excellent example of maintaining a cooperative spirit among so much diversity. Sixteen nations resonating in harmony, different backgrounds, cultures, skin colors, with one common denominator, Jesus Christ—this was diversity at its best.

By the power of God, I spoke life and encouragement into this congregation. I reminded the people that they had been trained and equipped to witness to those of their city who were not at all interested in Christianity.

I urged them to press forward in the strength of the Lord. I reassured them that it was not about numbers but about persistently showing God's love to those who do not obtain His treasure.

These believers were few, but very passionate for the Lord. We must continue praying that they do not become discouraged at the daunting task that lies before them.

This trip was not physically challenging, but it was, by far, the most spiritually challenging trip. The accommodations were nice, the hosts were marvelous, and the food was excellent. But the ever-present sense of negativity took its toll on my spirit.

On the plane ride home, one of my teammates, John Kelly, reflected over the many open-minded, amoral teens and college students we met while in Limoges. He said, "We are only one generation away from Americans adopting this way of believing."

We serve a mighty God who sacrificed His Only Son to transform our hearts and minds to reflect His heart and mind. When we obey Him and yield to His Authority, He gives us peace like a river and righteousness like the waves of the sea. It is imperative that American Christians believe this truth, bend their knees to His Sovereignty, and receive His gift of living a life reflecting Him. Otherwise, my friend's prediction will come to fruition.

Yes, in comparison to Asia, Africa, or South America, the harvest was small. However, God has not called us to be accountants or scorekeepers. One of those saved souls may be the next Paul, Billy Graham, or Mother Teresa. It is all in God's providence. It is not about our mission, because it is not our mission. We are invited to be a part of it. The mission, His mission, is to reconcile the world to Him. Praise His Holy Name, for He is allowing us to be a part of that.

Billy, Ludimilla, Manou, and Alain DuFour

CHAPTER 6

Saint Vincent

§

In January of 2013, the Lord opened up a door for me to return to Saint Vincent with three treasured friends: John Crunk, Larry Kunkle, and Charlie Earles, all novices.

While in flight, I began reminiscing about my first trip to Saint Vincent. In May of 2011, I had accepted the opportunity to go there with a group from Cookeville, Tennessee: Cecil, Jim, JP, and JP's wife, Lynda. First, I will tell you about our first trip.

Saint Vincent is a beautiful island. Our accommodations were fine, but there was no air conditioning in the hotel room, which forced us to sleep with the windows open. Throughout the night, I could hear God's creatures: dogs barking, frogs croaking, crickets chirping. Even louder than the creatures were the revelers outside my window. Sleep was impossible.

Our host church was Glen Baptist Church, pastored by thirty-seven-year-old Sylvester King. Pastor Sylvester was a charming man; he was small and quiet yet exuded a confident, committed character. He proved to be deeply motivated and highly skillful.

Sylvester was a bivocational man; he also worked in the government. His connections provided opportunities for us that we otherwise would not have had, such as witnessing in schools, sharing the Good News in a prison, meeting the president of the bar association, and proclaiming the Gospel on live national radio.

The publicity of this mission was so wide that I had become a household name even before I arrived. Because of my involvement in the Dr.

Martin Luther King Jr. case, I was an instant celebrity; many even considered me a hero. Dr. King is still very much an icon throughout the Caribbean.

Glen Baptist Church is large and has excellent acoustics. All its services, which have enormous turnouts, are broadcast on the radio. The first day, I gave a sermon entitled "The Rich Man and Lazarus." This parable is found in Luke 16:14–31: "Now is the time for salvation, for the gulf between Hades and Abraham's bosom is fixed. Once you breathe your last breath you receive a one-way ticket to an eternity of torment or to an eternity of delight."

Scores of people flooded the altar for various decisions. Pastor Sylvester and my team were impressed with the message, but I explained, "I've preached that sermon several times with no decisions. This is all God's doing."

The evening services at the church were filled to the brim. The musicians and singers were skilled at stirring the congregation with a spirit of worship and praise. Services usually lasted about two hours. I preached in a storytelling mode and then gave an invitation. Throngs of people responded; some wept tears of sorrow, some poured out tears of joy. The altar remained wet with tears at this church.

One morning, I was interviewed on the largest, most popular national radio station in Saint Vincent. The live interview was slated to be a thirty-minute discussion, but we talked nearly two hours. We spoke on a full range of subjects: the Dr. Martin Luther King Jr. case, politics, and civil rights. However, the emphasis of the interview was placed on Jesus Christ and the Good News He offers to all who accept Him as their Savior.

For lunch, I was taken to a mission's house. This beautiful and spacious home stood on pilings high atop a hill overlooking the Caribbean Sea. It had been purchased by a church member for the free use of missionaries.

We enjoyed the serene view of the placid Caribbean Sea as we dined. It was an extremely hot day, with a pleasant breeze offering some relief from the heat. A short nap revived and energized us for the rest of the day's activities.

While the others went on visitation, I stayed back at the mission's house to polish up a sermon for that evening's outdoor citywide revival. It was not long before Sylvester's wife, Cleopatra, and his mother-in-law came to speak with me. For well over an hour, they asked me questions about Dr. King. Everywhere I went, people were eager to get their fill of information on him.

That night, the setting was not at all to my liking. I stood on a protruding ledge on top of a thirty-foot-high hill while the people stood below me, lined up across the street. Cars drove between us. It was a massive crowd with people moving and stirring about.

I began telling a story, and a hush fell over the crowd. The movement and stirring ceased, and all became still. Those driving on the street moved at a snail's pace with their windows down, trying to catch a word or two.

At the conclusion, we sang, "I Surrender All," and the crowd sang out to the Lord with hands raised and eyes closed while swaying back and forth to the music. Sylvester went down to the people and gave an altar call. For forty-five minutes, the crowd responded to the Lord. Only the Lord knows the results of this unusual service.

The following day was gorgeous, with a refreshing, gentle breeze, blue skies, and puffy white clouds. Our morning was spent going door to door witnessing to people.

After lunch, I met with the president of the bar association, Dr. Lewis, and a prison official, Frankie. Dr. Lewis was a robust man, accustomed to being in charge. He fired off words like a machine gun as he shared a little about himself. He was a complex man with political ambitions. He was an idealist in many ways, but after conversing with him, I was confident that he was saved.

The next day, our team visited an antiquated prison that had been built to hold 82 men but at the time was housing 441 men and twenty women. Most inmates had been incarcerated for murder, rape, or other violent crimes. It was an unpleasant and appalling sight. The conditions were unsanitary and putrid, smelling of urine and feces.

Sylvester and Frankie accompanied me to the prison. The inmates were standing out in the yard, waiting for us. Frankie started things off with a short speech, reminding the prisoners to behave themselves and to listen. Sylvester followed up with a few songs. Some sang along, but most just had their arms crossed, glaring at us; the majority of the inmates seemed unmoved by these activities.

As I began sharing my testimony, the men became attentive; their eyes locked with mine, and their body language became more relaxed and open. These men sensed that I could relate to them and that I understood what they were going through. They realized I had something important to say, and they were not going to miss a word of it.

I shared with them the divine message of God's grace. "The perfect and innocent Son of God hung on a cruel cross to pay for your sins, for all of your crimes. Jesus gives this gift to all sinners. He gave the criminal next to Him on the cross access to heaven. No one is exempt from this free gift; not even the vilest offender. His gift of salvation is yours for the taking, if you just ask and receive."

Sixty-two men gave their lives to Christ.

We then stopped at a tiny, rickety shack and visited an unwed mother of five children. She eagerly gave her life to the One who promised never to leave or forsake her.

The following day, the Cookeville group set up at Glen Baptist Church, providing free eye exams and distributing reading glasses.

As the people were registering and waiting to have their eyes checked, Jim and I seized the moment, asking each person about his or her spiritual condition. One hundred twenty-five people had their eyes checked, seventy-eight received free reading glasses, and six accepted Christ as their Savior. God can use any place, any time, and any setting for us to go and tell His Good News.

We went back to the mission's house and supped on the back porch overlooking the emerald-green Caribbean waters, watching the sailboats effortlessly waft along. In the distance, I could see the red-tiled roof of the school we would embrace the next day.

The following morning, my team visited Rose Hall Government Elementary School. We each were placed in different rooms. I was positioned in a fourth-grade classroom with twenty-three boys and girls. I started out sharing the story of Jonah. They particularly liked the part where the big fish puked Jonah up onto the beach.

I closed with the following story: "A fourth-grade schoolteacher gave each of her students an empty plastic egg. Their project was to go outside and place something inside of the egg that showed new life. All the students eagerly took their eggs outside to find the perfect object that symbolized new life. Once they had completed the task, the children gathered around the teacher, who had placed the eggs in a basket. One by one, she pulled out eggs and revealed what was inside. One had a pretty little purple flower in it; another egg had a tiny yellow butterfly. But the next egg was empty. A shy little boy raised his hand and said, 'Teacher, that's my egg. I have new life because Jesus's tomb is empty.'"

This story settled the students' silliness, causing them to be much more serious. I then asked them, "How many of you believe Jesus's tomb was empty?" They all raised their hands. "If Jesus is not already your Lord and Savior, who would like to pray a prayer with me, asking Jesus into your heart so that you can have new life?" Two children prayed the sinner's prayer with me.

On our free day, we took a tour of the exotic, beautiful island of Saint Vincent. The elevation and sharp turns did not lend themselves to a comfortable ride; the drive would be a nightmare for anyone with motion sickness.

High upon a hill was an old fort lined with ancient cannons. The elevation was forty-five hundred feet, and it overlooked a vast view of the Caribbean. Some of the cannons dated back as far as the 1600s. The fort had been in active use up until World War II.

Later, we arrived at a lovely home of a prominent Saint Vincent family. We sat on the front porch enjoying the Caribbean breeze and the sweet fragrance of flowers. The couple's twenty-seven-year-old daughter, who was a high-school English teacher, joined us.

The family had heard me preach and enjoyed it so much that they discussed it late into the evening. As I sat there listening to them recap, word for word, my entire sermon and listening to their praises, I began to wonder why I had been called to visit this family. Surely, it was not to be praised and crowned with diadems.

As I continued listening, slowly, the reason began to emerge. The family was concerned about the twenty-one-year-old autistic son, Cameron. He was a computer genius and remarkable in many other ways. However, he seldom spoke and rarely shared his thoughts. This was a grave concern for the family in general, but specifically in regard to his salvation. They had no idea where he stood spiritually. Was he lost or saved?

At the mother's insistence, Cameron joined us on the porch. The conversation continued about him as though he was not present. He sat as still as a statue, stone quiet, staring at the floor.

Sylvester suggested I talk to Cameron privately, inside the house. I insisted that we all stay on the porch, because I felt that Cameron needed the security of his loving family around him and that he would not feel comfortable being alone with a stranger.

I pulled my chair up close to Cameron and began speaking to him softly. His face was expressionless. On occasion, he would nod, but at other times, he appeared obfuscated. When he did speak, his words were faint, barely audible.

I began sharing the EvangeCube with him. As I spoke about creation, he seemed indifferent. When I shared that Christ had died on the cross to save him from his sins, a furrow on his brow was noticeable as genuine concern spread across his face.

As I moved to the scene of the resurrection of Christ, I saw a gleam in his eye. It was as though clarity had struck deep within his soul. His face broke out into a rare yet radiant smile, bringing tears of unrepressed joy to the eyes of his family.

I asked Cameron if he would repeat the sinner's prayer after me. He answered in a strong, affirmative voice, "*Yes!*" He prayed without a stutter or a stammer; his prayer was clear, and concise.

That night, among a gentle Caribbean breeze and the sweet fragrance of Saint Vincent flowers, Cameron's name was written forever in the Lamb's Book of Life.

We did not have pomp and ceremony, liturgical exactness, or ecclesiastical splendor; we simply had fellowship with the Lord, right then and right there.

We are commanded to share His story at all times, in all seasons, and in all places. There is no proper setting, formula, or script. We are to live a surrendered life every day, all day. It is the Spirit within us who gives us the words to share during the divine appointments He puts into our day. It is not our strength, or our words, or our plan; it is His strength, His words, and His plan.

When we look into the mirror, we should see His face, dead to self, alive in Christ. The opportunities are abundant; we must seize them. Praying with your waitress, asking the Walmart cashier if he is saved, sharing Christ with the person standing behind you in line, making sure your family members' salvation is secure—the list goes on. Witnessing is not a suggestion; it is a command from the One Who created you and saved you. Do not let another opportunity slip away. Trust and obey.

§

Over the years, Sylvester and I had kept in touch. His church had grown, and so had his civil-service status. And so, a few years later, I flew back to Saint Vincent with my three buddies who were all eager to experience their first mission trip.

Let me take a moment to introduce you to my three friends. Each man has his own unique skills and gifts. John Crunk is a self-made, generous man who drives a hard bargain. He started his career as a stock boy but ended up owning a large office-supply company with a presence in several states and headquarters in Nashville, Tennessee. It was the only company he had ever worked for. He is semiretired.

Larry Kunkel also pulled himself up by the bootstraps, climbing to the pinnacle of the social and financial world. He has an inquisitive mind, yearning for knowledge. He was our theologian deal closer. His descriptive illustrations woo and wow listeners. His stories are personal, but always spiritually based, enriching the lives of those who listen.

Charlie Earles is the president of a successful company. He has a pleasant personality and would do anything for anyone. Charlie was our Norman Vincent Peale (a minister and the author of *The Power of Positive Thinking*). His motto is, "Smile, and the world smiles with you; cry, and you cry alone."

I did my best to prepare these men for the mission by introducing them to the EvangeCube, but I could tell from their eyes and facial expression that I had fallen short. I was looking forward to seeing Sylvester, hoping that his influence would inspire them and stir their spirit. I silently prayed, "Lord, show me the way and teach me today that You do what You say."

Sylvester met us at the airport. I was elated to reunite with him; his presence buoyed my spirits. Once again, he was a gracious host and well organized. He made sure we had a full schedule.

Our hotel accommodations were pleasant. We each had a private room with air conditioning, overlooking the Caribbean Sea. Downstairs was an open-air restaurant where we enjoyed many delicious meals. From the hotel, we went to Glen Baptist Church, where we were introduced to fifteen volunteers who steadfastly worked alongside us on the mission.

The next day, we were interviewed on the NBC affiliate that has the largest listening audience in Saint Vincent. The news was out all over town that we were there to spread the Gospel.

Our days were typically spent visiting in the slums, where alcohol abuse was prevalent. I worked with Pastor Sylvester, while Larry, John, and Charlie were teamed up with other seasoned veterans.

The following day, we visited Thomas Saunders Secondary School, speaking before an outside assembly of approximately five hundred kids. John, Larry, and Charlie each gave commendable presentations that kept the attention of the students. Several professions of faith were made.

The next morning, John and I met for breakfast, overlooking the Caribbean Sea. The gentle lapping of the waves soothed our ears, the redolence of the salty sea was pleasing, and the vision of the rising sun over the water was a sight to behold.

Our waitress, Harriet, took our order. I asked her, "Are you a Christian?"

"No, but I would like to be. I just don't know how," she said.

Right then and there, I laid out the plan of salvation for her. She admitted she was a sinner, believed Jesus died for her, confessed Him to be her Savior, and prayed the sinner's prayer with me.

From the breakfast table, I went to the front desk to ask for more towels. As I waited, I asked the two ladies behind the counter if they were Christians. They said they were not. After I explained the plan of salvation to them, they both accepted Christ as their Savior and prayed the sinner's prayer.

Three decisions had been made before we "officially" started our day.

We caught the van and went to Rose Hall Government Elementary School, the same one I had visited on my first trip to Saint Vincent. All the children were neatly dressed in their school uniforms. They sang their national anthem, said their pledge, and sang religious songs to us. Charlie, John, and Larry shared.

Afterward, we met with the school principal, who shared with us her concern for the financial needs of the children, with particular regard to affording books and lunches.

Our group discussed this matter privately, and after some thought and prayer, we made the decision to give the school $1,000.

Our next stop was to Saint Vincent Secondary School. It had been designed to educate and train troubled students. We met in a large assembly with about three hundred, all dressed nicely in their school uniforms. We each spoke, sharing the love and power of Jesus Christ. Approximately fifty students accepted Christ as their Savior.

That afternoon, we had the opportunity to share our faith with Ralph Gonsalves, the prime minister. He was a large, gregarious man, with a big belly laugh to match. He pontificated about his relationships with Fidel Castro, other world leaders, and various countries.

He claimed to be a Christian, though his beliefs and values did not reflect the fruit of the Spirit. I challenged him by saying, "It is God who put you in this lofty position, and because of your status you are held to a higher standard." He took the admonishment well.

At the end of the day, we had an evening youth rally. A popular band came and played for the youth, energizing and electrifying them.

Larry shared his moving testimony: "In my early Christian faith, I was encouraged to look deeply into my upbringing in the Christian Science Church, to examine the code of discipline I was given, and to reflect how that discipline equated to my sense of self-worth.

"I was challenged to ask myself if the message was a message of encouragement or a message that conveyed a negative attitude about who I was as a person.

"I discovered that I had been asked to live up to an image of perfection, which is a common core belief of the Christian Science Church. Of course, I did not always live up to this high standard, which caused me to feel like I had failed and that I was inferior.

"As a young adult, I began to realize that we, as humans, were born into an imperfect world, and that we inherited the sin nature of Adam. This freed me up to recognize that sin was something that we all shared, common to all people. Scripture instructs us that Jesus Christ paid the price for our sins with His blood on the cross.

"Out of this freedom came the belief that I had much to offer in the way of the Christian ministry. As I became familiar with the gifts of the Spirit, I learned that I did not have the gift of evangelism or the gift of healing, but I did have the gift of service.

"I strive to use this gift to help preachers and evangelists. I am daily led by the Holy Spirit to contribute to the Kingdom through service.

"I encourage all present at this service to examine your God-given strengths and to use them for the benefit of God's work in this world.

"We are all bricks in the giant wall of Christianity. It's important to know: we are loved by God, despite our imperfections; we are forgiven of all our sins through the blood of the lamb; we all have Spiritual gifts to be used for the glory of God."

Then John gave a motivational presentation about living a life of excellence. He encouraged the youth to have a dream, to make goals to achieve it, and to set a time frame to reach it.

"If the goal is not reached, that's OK. Reexamine your goal and start again. But never give up!"

Charlie wrapped things up with his rainbow story. He shared, "My wife, Carol, and I loved rainbows. We were always thrilled to spy one in the sky. Our favorite song was 'Somewhere Over the Rainbow.'

"One solemn day, my beloved bride went home to be with the Lord. What a dark and hopeless day. The next day, as I was on my way to pick up our son from the airport, the most splendid and spectacular rainbow lit up the sky, practically landing on my car. Peace that outshines all understanding flooded my heart and soul. I knew Jesus had sent this gift to me to brighten the black and despairing moment. It was as though the Prince of Peace was sending me a message, reassuring me that my sweet bride was in the presence of the Savior in paradise.

"Rainbows are a gift from God, a sign, a promise from Him that gives us hope and peace. This multicolored gift from God had a special meaning for me and Carol, and now, it has an even greater meaning to me.

"The emblem of the rainbow is a sign representing the victory of grace over judgment and the triumph of mercy over wrath. It is His insignia of love, patience, peace, and hope.

"We live in an age where it is important for us to go to the ends of the earth and tell of God. There will be a time when God shows His final act of wrath by destroying sinners by fire, and all unbelievers will perish.

"Next time you see a rainbow, recognize that you live under the arc of grace. When the storm passes and the sun is at our back, God's rainbow appears, radiating His patience and loving kindness.

"I enjoy painting rainbows and teaching others to paint them. His sign in the sky brings me comfort and joy." And he gave a painting demonstration.

Close to twenty youth came forward. I prayed over two who had been set aside to serve in mission work. All in all, it was our best day. Bone weary, we finally made it back to the hotel at 10:00 p.m.

The following day, we visited the same prison I had visited two years earlier. However, the population had downsized from 441 inmates to 250. A new prison had been built to house the more hardened criminals. The majority of the inmates in the older prison had been incarcerated for petty crimes.

Each of us took our turn speaking. I concluded by sharing my own prison experiences. About forty men accepted Christ.

That night, we ate at Pastor Sylvester's home, along with his lovely wife and mother-in-law. There was laughter, gaiety, and fun. The food was delicious.

We came back to the hotel around 9:00 p.m. It had been another long day. The crescendo would be the next day during the Sunday service.

The church was packed with people dressed in their very best. The music was fervent, loud, and moving. Pastor Sylvester began earnestly singing, producing a ripple effect that caused the congregation to sway their hands in unison; everyone seemed in the Spirit.

I preached on from the book of Acts. The audience was still, and I closed with a story. The invitation was given. Numerous people came forward, and buckets of tears flooded the altar. Some shed tears of repentance; others had tears of sorrow.

Perhaps the most precious and memorable person in attendance was a fifteen-year-old girl, Adriana, who found herself in the service that Sunday morning. It was her first time in church. John recognized that this shy girl was alone; he gently befriended her. During the invitation, she walked forward and gave her life to Jesus.

Shortly thereafter, John received this e-mail from Adriana:

i am askin u for sum prayers for me and my family. especially my mom who lost her sight and part of her foot. prayer for healing of her diabetes.

i'm askin for special prayers for me in my school work cuz i'm not doin that well. my teacher told me if my grades continue like that i would not be able to continue in her class. i need some prayers to study harder. thank you very much. God bless!

If she had been the only one saved on this mission, it would have been worthwhile. Jesus died for her.

The last words Jesus uttered on this earth can be found in Mark 16:15: "And He said unto them, go ye into all the world and preach the gospel to every creature."

This is the great commission; it is not a suggestion but a command. The clarion call of Christ is the same today as it was two thousand years ago.

Whom can I send?

What say you?

The Spirit showed up within each one of these men. God became our chief and led us for His glory. We were told that hundreds of people gave their lives to Christ in the slums, in the schools, over the radio, in the prisons, and maybe in high political places.

You might ask, "Why would you leave the comforts of home and go to a faraway place to minister when there is so much work to be done here?" That is a fair question. And so is this: "What have you done to advance the cause of Christ right here at home? Did you lead anyone to the Lord? Did you even speak His name to anyone?"

To end this chapter on a rather comical note, I will share a funny little incident from this trip. On our free day, John and Charlie took a stroll down the beach in their Speedos, much to the dismay of Larry and me. Their attire attracted the attention of some local ladies. Just before we departed the hotel for the airport, two attractive young ladies handed John and Charlie each a decorative gift bag adorned with a silver bow. Inside was a new, bright-red Speedo suit with the words *St. Vincent* written across the rear end. The guys would certainly make a fashion statement in Destin and be the envy of all who saw them.

Three men saved in the ghetto

John Crunk, Billy Gray, Larry Kunkle, Charlie Earles

CHAPTER 7

Orissa, India

$

THE TRAIN TUGGED ALONG WITH all its might, making its way up and around the mountains as we headed to Orissa, a state just north of Andhra Pradesh, India. The terrain was breathtaking. A variety of flowers were in bloom, and the vegetation and trees were at their peak.

I sat by the window, absorbing a landscape of India I had never seen before while sitting among the rest of the lower-caste people. I heard the cries of fussy children and mothers scolding them as well as the sounds of bleating sheep. A goat walked past me down the aisle, as though he was collecting tickets. The smells of body odor, animals, and defecation infiltrated my nose. The lowered windows allowed cool air to circulate, bringing a blessed relief from the smells.

Despite all the distractions within the train, the view without made the ride tranquil. I did not want the peaceful moment to end, for I knew there would be immense challenges ahead.

As our group exited the train, we saw vendors gathered around, loudly hawking their fare of horribly foul and smelly food. The bathrooms were so repugnant, I gagged upon entering. There was no sanitation to be found.

We walked nearly a mile before reaching our sublime accommodations: little one-bedroom cottages, with a dining room and a meeting hall. On the first evening, our team met the locals and our interpreters. This was usually a festive occasion, but that night, the atmosphere seemed ghoulish.

After a little time and some patience, the reason for the eerie sense began to reveal itself as the locals opened up to us. In an area where violence was nearly unheard of, brutality had reared its ugly head. A leper had attacked a shepherd boy, beating him nearly to death. His young life hung in the balance.

The same day, a girl had heard her dogs barking and went to investigate the ruckus. The dogs were chasing after a bear. The bear had turned and attacked her, breaking her jaw with one swipe of his paw.

The superstitious people in this community believed a blanket of evil had been draped over it. Many believed that we, the Christians, had brought this evil onto them and that we should not be there. Our Indian leaders grew less and less optimistic about this mission.

Our team began to reason together. Maybe we should leave and go back to Visakhapatnam. If we stayed, would we be safe from attack as we walked along isolated paths in the rural area? Many of the people were looking at us as though we were evil spirits out to do them harm. What would the villagers do to protect their village from strange, white Christians?

These questions flooded our minds, but we had no answers. We fell to our knees and asked the One Who was in control to lead, guide, and direct us. We asked Him to reveal His will to us and to be a light unto our feet.

The next day, my interpreter, George, and I set out on our own journey, visiting other villages within the same area. There were no roads leading to these villages, just narrow, dusty paths. Each village was approximately a mile apart, set back a hundred yards from the path and behind dense trees. Only people familiar with the location knew these villages even existed. Once inside the villages, we were invisible to the rest of the world and fully reliant upon Our Protector.

We exited the dense trees, and before us opened up a village. Small, naked children playing outside of a hut noticed us and quickly ran inside. We approached the closed door, and George knocked. No answer.

He knocked louder a second time and called out in Telugu, "Hello? Is anyone there?"

Finally, after a long pause, a small, frightened female voice answered George in Telugu, "We are afraid the white man will bring us harm. Go away!"

As I started to enter another village, George cried, "No, no, Brother Bee-lee!" He explained to me that this village was demon possessed. The people drank all day and constantly fought one another. The children did not go to school, and they had no clothes. As I peered into the village, I could feel the oppressive spirit of evil pass over me. Even the dogs were fighting. It reminded me of Nineveh.

As George and I walked on, I wondered if the reaction we had received so far was a harbinger of what we were to expect for the remainder of the trip. Had our two years of detailed planning been for naught? The servants on this mission had spent their own hard-earned money, and supporters had given generously. Many were using their vacation time for the mission, a trip of a lifetime. How could this be? Had we traveled all this way, spent all this money, used all this time, just to have doors closed to us?

A still, small voice whispered to my conscience, reminding me that this was all in His control and on His timetable. Even our most righteous plans can differ from God's. He had the right to redirect us. Often, God uses us the most when we feel the least adequate. Maybe we were right where He wanted us.

The following day, George and I visited a village with a one-room Christian school. The twenty-five students, ages six to sixteen, were so neatly dressed in their school uniforms, they could have passed the tightest inspection of a drill sergeant. They sang "Jesus Loves Me" in Telugu with such a joyous sound that I was certain the heavenly angels gave them a standing ovation. Afterward, each student quoted a passage of Scripture with accuracy and confidence. What a refreshing time I had with these young, eager believers.

I stepped outside of this heavenly haven into a world of stark contrast, where poverty and ignorance reigned supreme. Roaming about like rudderless ships were naked children with their drunken mothers.

Many of these children were of school age, but their parents did not want them educated.

Some of the families allowed us to come into their huts and accepted God as their newfound Hope. There was no church meeting or mass gathering; it was all done within the tiny confines. There was no grand hurrah, but there was great rejoicing in heaven over these repentant sinners, and all the glory went to God.

The next day, eight of us crammed into a six-passenger van to a fishing village adjacent to Visakhapatnam, the village where George had grown up. We enjoyed the respite from the oppressive heat and delighted in the beauty of nature surrounding us, but our spirits were heavy laden by the overwhelming, oppressive evil that surrounded us. Very little joy was on the drive. Some were battling feelings of defeat, while others were fighting motion sickness.

God's spectacular creation was just as magnificent going back up as it was coming down. George was the city librarian and very well educated. He provided us with a running commentary on each tree, flower, and bush that we passed. He was so informative on this subject, I suspected he could have been a horticulturist.

As we approached George's village on the Bay of Bengal, he told of the devastating tsunami that had engulfed the fishing village in 2004. The area looked as though a massive hand had come in and pushed everything back as far as the eye could see. We were not prepared to see such vast destruction. We were left stunned and shocked by the bareness of the land. It was such a difference from the beautiful, fertile land we had just seen.

George then pointed over to the plains where a village had once stood; it had been completely wiped off the face of the earth. But there was far more to this story than just the annihilation of a village. George regaled us with the miraculous tale:

A small minority of two hundred Christians once lived under the leadership of a professing Hindu chieftain. One Friday afternoon, the Christians asked permission from the chief to travel to the mountains for a weekend celebration of their Christian faith. The chief refused their request, and they were disappointed, yet they bent their knees to the Chief of All Chiefs and continued to pray.

Later, that same afternoon, the chief changed his mind and gave the Christians permission to take their pilgrimage to the mountains as long as they agreed to come back by Sunday afternoon. They accepted this condition.

All Christian men, women, and children ventured to the mountaintop. Without any warning, early Saturday morning, a tsunami came crashing over the land, causing chaos, destroying property, and claiming lives. The chief and his villagers were washed away, never to be seen again. The Christians on the mountaintop were saved.

The surrounding villagers began seeing Christianity with new eyes. God said, "He would never leave us nor forsake us." The surviving Christians used this miraculous story to encourage others to accept Jesus as their Lord and Savior.

Touched by this story, I asked this prolific interpreter to tell me his story of salvation. "Oh, that's easy, Brother Bee-lee. It was my grandfather. When he was sixteen years old, he attended a meeting conducted by a white man from the United States of America. He must have been like you, Brother Bee-lee."

The white man had shared John 14:6: "Jesus answered, I am the way and the truth and the life. No one comes to the Father except through Me." Grandfather knew something was missing in his life and that he wanted to live in heaven. He went forward publicly professing Jesus as his Lord and Savior.

"Grandfather was so happy, he ran and skipped all the way home. Bursting with joy, he shared this good news with his family. Much to his chagrin, though, his devout Hindu family was untouched by this truth and demanded he renounce the silly notion immediately. Despite Grandfather's youth, he stood steadfast on his newfound convictions.

"Grandfather was accused of being an unworthy and belligerent son. He was told that he must reclaim the Hindu tradition, or he would be cast out of the home with just the clothes on his back.

"Grandfather was shattered by his family's response, yet he knew he had heard the truth. Abandoned by his earthly father, he clung to the truth that his Heavenly Father would never leave nor forsake him.

"Grandfather turned to leave, but his father called him back under the guise of offering him a parting gift. It was a gift that lasted a lifetime: his father took a blazing-hot poker and seared Grandfather's lips, permanently scarring him.

"Although young and inexperienced, Grandfather persevered and became one of the wealthiest men in this part of India. Years later, my father was born, who is also a Christian. I am one of four sons. We are all in Christian ministry.

"I don't remember ever seeing my grandfather's faith waver, neither have I ever heard him express bitterness over the past. So, Brother Bee-lee, it is because of Grandfather that I became a Christian."

With this amazing story of faith fresh on my mind, I woke up early Sunday morning with eager anticipation of preaching at George's home church. As we walked to it, I found the village reminiscent of Destin, Florida, in the 1950s. Commercial boats were tied to the docks, and the seawater lapped against the hulls, making a rhythmic sound. It was a quiet, peaceful, Sunday morning with no blaring horns or hustle and bustle in the streets.

As we approached, I was stunned by the beautiful architecture of the building. It reminded me of a "high church," one that favors formality. Inside, the pulpit sat far above the pews, two royal-looking high-backed chairs for the speakers to sit in while waiting their turn to speak.

The center section was divided into male and female sections. To the left of the pulpit were pews that faced the center section, reserved for the high-caste males. The back of the church was of primarily clear-glass windows through which I could see the Bay of Bengal and the docked boats while standing at the pulpit. I was introduced to the preacher, who was just like the church: very formal. He was courteous and polite but as stiff as a freshly starched shirt.

Before the service began, I asked one of our team members, Jody, to come up and sit with me on the platform. It was my intention for this spirit-filled co-servant to share her testimony before I delivered my sermon. I quickly found out that this was an egregious mistake and would certainly not be allowed. Women were not allowed upon the platform or to sit in the "throne" chairs. However, Jody was allowed to stand on the floor to share her testimony.

The shabby treatment of Jody enraged me. My nostrils flared, and the veins in my neck bulged. She deserved respect. Jody, however, responded with grace and dignity, giving her testimony from the floor without the slightest bit of offense as I sat high above her on the platform in a throne chair.

Though her testimony could have broken through to the hardest heart, the church, like the pastor, had a coldness and a dullness of spirit. I suppose that was to be expected in a caste-system society, a place where women were not valued even among fellow believers.

The pastor then announced that one of the members would sing a special song that he had written himself. A distinguished older man with snow-white hair rose and stood facing the congregation on the floor below the pulpit. He began singing his song with a rich, melodious voice in Telugu. The words were his words and in his language but to the old, familiar hymn, "Have Thine Own Way Lord."

The Spirit was flowing freely like a gentle breeze at sunset. A metamorphosis was taking place. The congregation was coming alive, swaying back and forth to the song.

The upright, older gentleman turned toward me and bowed graciously. And then I saw it: the seared lips. The grandfather! With my heart swelling and my eyes filled with tears, I looked directly at George, who gave me a proud smile and two thumbs up. The ear-to-ear grin on his face said, "That's my grandfather!"

The grandfather stood for all that was good. He was the yeast in the dough, the salt in the world, the light in the darkness.

Well, this mission had not been what we'd hoped for and far from what we had planned. Our numbers did not meet our expectations, and our goals seemed to be unmet. But maybe, just maybe, some little boy we met will live for Jesus, becoming like the grandfather.

From some of the locals' perspective, our arrival seemed like a blanket of evil upon their community. From our view, our service appeared to be in vain. But I am confident that God was looking down below from His throne chair in heaven, seeing His Gospel spread out like an all-encompassing comforter. The seeds have been planted. Now the rest is up to the Holy Spirit, and all the glory and honor will go to the Lord.

Billy and Jody

George's brother, Billy, and George

CHAPTER 8

Honduras

§

OUR GAME PLAN FOR HONDURAS was perfect. Marge and I were to take a noon flight to Atlanta, staying the night in the Hilton hotel. Then we were to have a nice meal and a good night's rest, assuring that we would be fresh as daisies the next day.

There were seventeen people from different parts of the United States going to Honduras; we would all meet in Atlanta first. We had thirteen people well into their seventies and four people in their eighties; one man was in a wheelchair.

Often, though, game plans change. No matter how well you prepare, you really never know what lies ahead on a mission trip. You must just press on and trust in Him. The entire trip was one plan change after the next.

The next day, we boarded a plane with the smell of fresh leather seats. We were right on time and some of the first people to board. As we prepared to take off, a flight attendant made an announcement: "There is an electrical problem. It should only take a few minutes to fix."

Well, a few minutes turned into two hours. Finally, the attendant announced, "Ladies and gentlemen, I'm sorry, but the situation could not be resolved. For your safety, we need you to exit the plane. There will be another flight available later this afternoon." We unloaded our belongings and made the trek back to the terminal.

After shuffling flights around, we finally arrived at the chaotic Honduras airport, where our luggage was loaded onto the back of a pickup truck and covered with a tarp.

We were ushered onto a retired school bus filled with seats made for small children; my knees were practically up under my chin. After a three-hour drive, we arrived at our hotel. I was thankful my room had air conditioning and a modest bathroom.

We had our share of hardships on this trip. Each night, after working twelve-hour days, we came back to the hotel hot and sweaty, smelling like goats but unable to shower because there was no water.

We often missed meals, because the church was unable to provide lunch for us, and the hotel dining room was closed by the time we finished our days. When we did get a meal, our choice of food never changed. We consistently ate chicken, rice, corn, and fruit.

On our first day, we went to orientation, where Marge and I met Pastor Molina and Victor, our interpreter. Pastor Molina was the earthly shepherd of a small church with thirty-six members. He was a compassionate man with a big smile and an even bigger heart.

The next day, Pastor Molina picked us up in a nice car with air conditioning. The drive to the village was about twenty minutes from our hotel. The afternoon was hot, and the streets were dusty. The villagers lived in squalor and were impoverished. But there was joy amid their poverty. It was as if they did not know they were so disadvantaged.

Most homes in the village had only one room, about eight by twelve feet. Few homes had electricity, and no one had indoor plumbing. The children played in the dirt streets until after dark. They kicked balls, rode bicycles, and rolled inner tubes with sticks. Young children ran around naked. But no children or adults went around with their heads down, staring at a handheld device.

I was then taken to the church, which was nice, but it was also very noisy with many distractions. It had only one large room that was sectioned off for different small groups. As I was preaching, babies squalled in one corner of the room, and the children's Sunday-school class was held next to the pulpit. It was difficult preaching amid the noise and confusion. The disorder was frustrating to me, and to top it off, Victor was a horrible interpreter.

The next day was a delightful morning without a cloud in the sky and a cool, gentle breeze. The villagers brought chairs out, and we all sat underneath a shade tree. The women baked, washed, and tended to the babies.

There were no appointments scheduled, so the villagers took it upon themselves to entertain me; a guitarist played and sang. Later that afternoon, I was able to make some visits and lead people to Christ. By the end of the evening, our team counted a total of forty-three decisions made.

The following night, I had the most unusual experience. The church was more attentive than usual. There were no babies crying, no distractions, and the interpreter was on cue. I preached a sermon that I had preached many times before with scores of commitments made. But not this night. It was as though the people were in shock. I asked, "If you are sure of your salvation, raise your hand."

No hands went up.

Then I asked, "If you are unsure of your salvation, raise your hand."

Again, no hands.

Then I said, "May God have mercy on your souls."

Victor just looked at me and shrugged, not knowing why no one was responding.

I went back to the hotel room frustrated and disappointed. By the time I got to the dining room, the kitchen was closed. My body was slowing down, the heat was penetrating, and my spirit was sagging. The extreme temperature was wearing on the entire team.

The following day, we visited a private home, holding church in the backyard. A refreshing breeze revived us and buoyed our spirits. Marge spoke on what a friend we have in Jesus.

The good news of the cross and resurrection was received with as much joy as a toy on Christmas morning. The people there reveled in the phrase, "He included me."

On our fourth day, I explained to Pastor Molina that we had missed supper on the previous nights. He assured me that he would provide us transportation to the hotel in time to eat. After eleven hours of service under the blazing-hot sun and the high humidity of Honduras, we completed our services. Pastor Molina dismissed us and escorted us to the car that was waiting to take us back to the hotel for a much-needed meal.

It is rather difficult to describe the car, if you could even call it that. It was a Frankensteinian car, if you will, a hodgepodge of parts of different cars put together to make some semblance of a vehicle. The rear fenders were from a 1962 baby-blue Cadillac; the rest of the car had chipped black paint with rust holes large enough to stick a fist through. The hood ornament was from a 1946 Hudson Hornet, the classic triangular swoop. The steering wheel was from a Volkswagen.

At this point, we were so tired and hungry that we did not care how we got back to the hotel, as long as we got back in time to eat. But as it turned out, the outrageous appearance of this car was not to be our only shock. Marge pulled on the door to get into the back seat. The door would not budge, so she walked around the car and tried the other door but got the same result.

The driver sheepishly said something to Victor. He reported to us in English, "The back doors do not open. To get into the back seat, you must crawl through the window." Words cannot describe the look of mortification on Marge's face. This modest, poised, fine Christian lady wearing a mid-knee skirt looked at me as if to say, "You have got to be kidding me!"

She put her arm around my shoulder and hiked her leg up onto the window sill. Then she wrapped her other arm around Pastor Molina. Marge boosted her other leg up onto the window sill, all the while saying to me, "My skirt, my skirt! Pull my skirt down!"

She balanced herself in the open window, pulled down her skirt, and rested a moment with her arms on top of the car with a look of disgust on her face. She took a deep breath, slowly let it out, and then slid into the back seat. As she slid down, she hit her head on the door frame, causing her neatly arranged bun to droop off to the side of her head like an extra appendage. If looks could kill, I would have died on the spot.

I opened the passenger-side door with its mirror dangling off like a wet noodle. It bumped up against the door as I opened it. As I went to take my seat, I saw that the glove box was open, so I reached down to shut it. But it flopped back open again. With a little more gusto and a lot more aggravation, I attempted to shut the glove box again—to no avail. I slid into my seat and held the glove-box door shut with my knees jammed up into the dashboard because the seat would not readjust. Within seconds, I felt as though I was suffocating. I attempted to roll down my window, but the crank was missing.

Our driver got into the contraption and started her up. The entire car shook like a cheap hotel's vibrating bed. If I had not known I was in a car, I would have thought I was on a tractor with the intense juddering and racket. Just when we thought we were finally on our way, the driver announced that the lights were not working. "Wonderful," I ruminated.

All the elders of the village came to our rescue. They surrounded the car and discussed how to solve the dilemma. After much debate, they departed, and each one came back with a different tool: a wrench, a screwdriver, a hammer, a tire iron, and a jack. I am no mechanic, but this didn't look promising.

Each elder took a shot at the car with his tool of choice. Shockingly, nothing worked! So these wise sages decided to change a tire. What a tire had to do with an electrical problem I had no idea, but nevertheless, this is what they chose to do. The replacement tire had not seen tread since Harry Truman's victory lap in 1945. Astonishingly, changing the tire did not make the lights work!

These sagacious men then called a taxi to liberate us from the village of vexation. We were informed that it would take two hours for the taxi to reach the remote village.

With a look of total disgust on her face, Marge climbed back out of the car window. With gracious dignity, she smoothed out her skirt and brushed back a piece of hair from her face, leaving the dangling bun as though it was meant to be there.

By this time, a real crowd had surrounded us. The spectators were quite amused by Marge's accomplishments. Moments later, a fourteen-year-old boy rode up on his motor scooter. He opened the car's hood and wiggled the wires connected to the headlights. Voilà, on came the head-lights. This took less than thirty seconds.

I was grateful for the boy's intuitive skill; however, I knew this meant Marge had to climb back through that window. As we shoved her in, her modesty went out. On the other hand, she received a standing ovation from the vast crowd that surrounded us. I resumed my place, securing the glove box with my knees. We finally began the journey back to the hotel.

The windshield was so disfigured that I could not even see the Hudson Hornet hood ornament. The driver had to peek through a tiny space be-tween the cracks to see the road. The floor beneath my feet had a baseball-size hole through which I could see the road passing underneath us. The exhaust permeated the inside of the car, creating smoke so thick that I could not see Marge or Victor in the back seat.

The potholes on the highway were big enough to swallow an entire car. The driver weaved in and out between the gaping holes like someone driving an obstacle course around cones. We were often in the lane of on-coming traffic. The dexterity of the car was subpar, causing us to narrowly avoid head-on collisions.

The back driver's side wheel clipped a smaller pothole, causing us all to bounce so high that we hit our heads on the ceiling of the car. It landed with such a tremendous impact that a back door fell right off its hinges into the highway.

"Egad!" Marge shouted.

I hollered back, "Marge, are you OK?"

She answered, "*No!* This is perfectly horrible!"

I have never prayed so hard in my life!

Finally, we arrived at the hotel with shouts of victory, praise, and ap-plause. It was akin to when a plane lands on American soil after a long, hard flight to a third-world country.

Marge slid across the back seat and stepped out of the hole that once had had a door. Her eyes were as big as saucers, and she was as white as a ghost. Needless to say, we went to bed without supper again that night. We were too exhausted to be hungry anyway.

For those of you who say you are too old or that time has passed you by, this story is proof that neither is true. All seventeen people on this trip were over the age of seventy-five, and we all survived. God delights in using the old, weak, ineffective, and disabled. He always leads us in triumph, which brings glory to Himself (2 Corinthians 2:14).

The Lord's question has never changed: "Whom shall I send and who will go for us?"

Honduras was horrendously hot and horribly humid. But this was a trip where David slew Goliath. Our Lord was the victor, as 3,293 souls were added to His ever-increasing army.

Some mission trips are filled with great harvests, some have amazing miracles, and some are spiritually challenging, while others are physically demanding. Some trips are life challenging, and others are just comedy skits that only the Lord could write. This mission trip was of the comedy variety.

Beach house

CHAPTER 9
Chile

§

Do you remember a time when you were young and falling in love was so easy? On a piece of paper, you would write, "Will you go with me? Circle yes or no." Then you would neatly fold the note and pass it to the one you hoped loved you back. This is how easy it was for me to fall in love with the Chileans. I immediately circled yes!

It had just been two short months since terrorists flew planes into the Twin Towers in New York, crashed a plane into the Pentagon and another in Pennsylvania (events now known infamously as the 9/11 attacks). The plane to Chile from the United States was nearly empty. Americans were still apprehensive about flying. However, the airport in Chile was bustling with people ready and eager to fly.

Originally, I was to go to Santiago, a more temperate climate. But things changed after my travels began, and I was sent to Punta Arenas, which is twelve hundred miles south of Santiago. It is the end of the world; the southernmost tip of Chile.

My dear friend and mentor, Dr. James Monroe, taught me to always be ready for change. I willingly accepted the change of venue but had not packed for the cooler climate. Even though it was springtime in the States, it was bone chillingly cold, with snow on top of the mountains surrounding us in Chile. Punta Arenas was considered a big resort area good for hiking and camping. It was situated on the Magellan Straits, good for fishing and shipping businesses.

The Chilean Baptist Church had invited me and my group to work with their pastors and churches. My team consisted of two men in their eighties from Colorado, two women in their sixties from Arizona, and our sweet, eighteen-year-old interpreter, Jazmyne.

My Western team members had a hard time understanding my Tennessee accent. They asked Jazmyne how she could understand it. She laughed and said, "He is easy to understand. I studied English at the University of Tennessee for six months. It is you that I have trouble understanding."

During the days, we split up, knocking on doors and presenting the plan of salvation to the unsaved. I had long been accustomed to preaching before audiences of various sizes, but this was my first time "cold calling." This was how they did it in Chile, and so, once again, I adjusted. I was pleased and surprised to get such gracious reception from the residents. These were some of the most loving and kind people I had ever met.

We visited a very humble home of an older lady. She opened the door and invited us into her nearly bare home. She was wearing a thick wool ski cap, a heavy coat, and a scarf. If possible, I think it was colder inside her house than it was outside. The few furnishings she had were old and worn out. Springs jutted out of the love seat cushions. As she reached behind her curtain to pull out an orange crate to sit on, the frail little lady told us her name was Rosa.

She began telling us that her husband was a sailor and had been away from home for nearly a year. For six months, she had not heard from him. Also, she had not received the monthly allotment he had always faithfully sent to her while he was away. Just days before, she had been told her husband's ship was destroyed in a storm off the coast of the Pacific Ocean but that he had survived the wreck and would be home soon.

Despite the good news, it was as though an anvil of fear had fallen upon her as she shared this with us. For six long months, she had had no idea if he was dead or alive. She was grateful that her husband would be home soon, but the months of worry had taken a great toll on her. She knew it would be months before he would be able to work again, and this was their only source of income. She was thin from little food and great anxiety. Her voice trembled as she told us her story.

I then began explaining the good news of the Gospel to her. She could not believe that Jesus could love a poor, old woman like herself. It was unthinkable to her that Jesus died for her. I shared John 3:16: "For God so loved the world that He gave His Only Son, Jesus, that whoever believes in Him will not perish but will have everlasting life."

Rosa's tiny frame rested in my arms, quivering and sobbing. A metamorphosis began taking place before my very eyes. The haggard look and hopeless eyes were replaced with a sparkle and a radiance that probably had not crossed her face since her wedding day.

A meager home with no electricity, no heat, and an empty cupboard had just been visited by the King of kings. The High Potentate had come to visit Rosa that day and lovingly wrote her name down in the Lamb's Book of Life. It was later reported to me that a "good Samaritan" had filled her cupboard with food and paid her rent for several months.

On the last day, the pastor asked me to visit an unsaved, unwed teenage mother. She had run away from home and was living on the streets when she became pregnant. She had no place to go, so she returned home and gave birth to a baby girl.

The young mother moved gingerly, as though she had had a very difficult delivery and was still in a great deal of pain. Her attention, however, was fixed upon my every word. She listened carefully and thoughtfully as the plan of salvation and the hope of forgiveness was explained to her. I emphasized the importance of bringing her little girl, Mia, up in a Christian home and how becoming part of a church could garner her the support and help she needed. She accepted the Lord as her Savior. She then asked if I would dedicate her daughter to the Lord that night at church. I agreed. The grandmother offered to bring the child, since the young mother was still recovering.

Each night I spent preaching to a full house at the local church. The final night was the most crowded. People stood in all the open spaces. As it came time for me to dedicate baby Mia, I was amazed to see the young mother in attendance. When the presentation time came, Mia's mother gently carried her down the aisle. The four-day-old baby girl lay snuggled in her arms as she came up onto the platform.

With the power of God, nothing is impossible. By His power, she witnessed the dedication of her daughter unto Him. Peace and joy radiated in the mother's face despite her physical pain.

I was so grateful for Jazmyne and her accuracy and ability to translate my southern accent. With Jazmyne, I could speak and have full confidence in her translation. One evening, there was some confusion in the order of speakers. A Chilean teacher was assigned to be my interpreter as Jazmyne sat listening in the audience. Once again, I adjusted.

Immediately, I could feel the anticipation of this new interpreter. I shared with the congregation how Joseph was sold into slavery by his brothers to Potiphar and how Potiphar's wife tried to seduce Joseph, causing him to be falsely accused and imprisoned. Despite Joseph's trials, he continued to persevere and trust in God. In the end, he prevailed.

As I was preaching, I could tell by the strange facial expressions of the congregation that something was wrong, just like when a musician hits a sour note. After the service concluded, Jazmyne approached me and told me that the translation had gone awry. The interpreter had said that Joseph was sold to a prophet, and then he had attacked the prophet's wife. Jazmyne and I did our best to explain the mistake to as many people as we could before they walked out the door.

One day, I had the opportunity to speak with four different highschool classes. The students had many interesting questions for me: Are all Americans Baptist? Is Thanksgiving just for Baptists? Are people born Baptist? As you might suspect, many of these students were Catholic. They also asked questions about cloning: Do farmers clone their animals? Was I a clone? Do Americans clone servants?

Then the inevitable subject of 9/11 came up. The students seemed to believe our calamity had been based on God's judgment upon the United States. This saddened me, but there was little I could say or do to change their minds. I told them that God is just, and even though our human justice system breaks down, God's justice system does not.

After I listened to them, they, in turn, listened to me share the Gospel of Salvation. Many claimed Christ to be their Lord and Savior.

Despite our communication barrier, the warmhearted Chileans repeatedly expressed their love and concern for me. It was such a joy and a privilege to share Christ's love with these open and receptive people. The Chileans taught me more than I taught them.

I was reminded that well-organized plans may change throughout the course of a trip, but His plans are etched in stone. As Christ followers and bondservants, we are to continue steadfastly on with the plans He has in store for us. We are not to lean on our own understanding but fully trust Him with all of our hearts. He will prevail, indeed!

Pastor, Billy, and Jazmyne

CHAPTER 10
India, 2012

§

SOME MISSION TRIPS ARE FILLED with great harvests of new believers, healings, and even miracles. Other trips can seem like uneventful chores. This particular one fell somewhere between those two categories.

Each day was filled with physical, emotional, and spiritual hurdles. This made it difficult to see the bounty and to focus on the reason I was there. I was there to share His truth with the lost and to encourage and train pastors to continue fighting the good fight.

The trip was marked by a raw attitude, endless travel, added and unexpected expenses, rushing and waiting, inedible food, sleepless and cold nights, poor organization, and bad decisions. However, in the end, God prevailed. None of this was a surprise to Him; He was the One in control.

As I battled a churning stomach within the confines of an airplane for fifteen hours from Newark, New Jersey, to Delhi, India, I wondered if it was an indicator of the course of the mission. This was not a good way to start a trip, especially to India.

Before departing from the States, I had been assured that a national had agreed to pick me up from the Delhi Airport and take me to the Raviz Hotel. Then I would meet the rest of the team, and we would fly together to Hyderabad the following day.

However, my promised ride was a no-show. I was not given a number or an address for the hotel. No one in the airport had heard of the Raviz. I exited the airport and found a Days Inn to rest for the night, trusting God to work out the details the next day.

The next morning, I walked back to the airport with my luggage in tow. It was a strange feeling to be in a foreign country all on my own, with no connection with people I knew and unable to communicate with the locals. All I could do was forge on and trust in God.

I found my terminal, boarded the plane, and sank into my seat. I breathed a sigh of relief when I looked up and saw the mission's leader, Steve, and the team boarding the plane. We flew three hours to Hyderabad and then drove two hours, packed into a bus like sardines, to Vijayawada. Each bump in the road made my stomach feel like waves churning in the sea.

After dropping our luggage off at the Hotel Raj Towers, we went straight into our meeting. We received glowing reports of the effectiveness of the mission in progress. Steve was impressed.

We ate at Joseph's house for lunch. He was on furlough, visiting his family. His ministry was to Indians who had immigrated to the United States. Fortunately, he served roast chicken, which my sensitive stomach could handle. But the rest of the food was an irritant to me. I was grateful for the added protein and for Joseph's hospitality.

The next day, Joseph picked me up, and we drove three hours to Rajahmundry, arriving at a service already in progress. I spoke a word of encouragement to the congregation. My Chicago-trained interpreter did an excellent job with an added flair of humor.

The church graciously prepared a feast for us, but I was unable to eat. My stomach still felt as though it was on the high seas. At the conclusion of the event, I was told that Joseph was not able to drive me back to the hotel, yet no other provisions had been made for my return. This forced me to hire a taxi at an exorbitant expense.

I was grateful to be in bed to rest and reflect. I was mentally drained, physically hungry, and emotionally exhausted. The next day, I was supposed to preach, but I had no idea where or to whom I would be preaching.

Poor management and bad decision making was frustrating me. I tried to focus on His provision and trust in His perfect planning and timing. "Go with the flow," I reminded myself. My stomach needed some relief, but all had come to a standstill. The rest of my body seemed to be hyper accelerated. My heart was beating a little faster, and my mind was racing.

Steve and I met for breakfast—another inedible meal. Our driver was late picking us up. I asked God to forgive me for my bad attitude and to give me an attitude adjustment so that frustration did not infiltrate my spirit. After all, this was all about Him and not about my comfort or my timing.

Just before leaving, Steve and I found out that we were speaking to children in the morning and adults later in the day. Even though we arrived late to the first church, no one was there. Nearly an hour later, ten children arrived. Pam and Steve used a flip chart to teach the life story of Jesus. The children enjoyed the pictures and the story. Roz, the interpreter, did a wonderful job and was very animated. The children adored her.

Our next destination was to Roz's church, where I would be presenting the Gospel. We loaded all ten children up and took them with us to the next church. I was beginning to feel like a day-care service more than a missionary. I gave a short message to an audience of several more children. Once again, Roz's energetic interpretation captured the children's attention, and they were engrossed in the story.

Afterward, we went to a muddy pond, where seventeen children were baptized. We then transported the original ten children back to their church.

Steve and I then both spoke to a congregation of adults. Eighteen accepted Jesus and repeated the sinner's prayer. We rushed back to the hotel, a forty-five-minute drive, to check out just in time. We only had ten minutes to spare so as not to incur extra charges. "Hurry up and wait, hurry up and wait" seemed to be the theme. We ate lunch, which I barley nibbled on, exchanged money, and drove for two hours to Kakinada.

There was an enormous amount of travel on this trip and a lot of changing hotels. It made it difficult to focus on the mission at hand. The roads were horrendous and taxing on the body. The drivers were reckless, which rattled my nerves.

The second hotel was not as nice as the first, but it was adequate. I was relieved to finally be able to hang up my clothes and settle in a little. I laid my head down on the pillow and praised God for His mercy. I was looking forward to a good night of sleep and much-needed rest.

However, it was a sleepless and restless night. The local Indians stayed up all night, talking and laughing in the streets outside of my hotel room until the early hours of the morning. As soon as I drifted off to sleep, I would be jostled awake by voices.

Again, I attempted to focus on God and His favor, trying not to make this about me and my comfort. His One and Only Son suffered far more imaginable discomforts than I would ever experience in a lifetime.

At 6:00 a.m., a young man knocked at my door, offering me a bucket of hot water. I was clueless as to why he was offering this to me. When I declined, he gave me a strange look. He showed me a washcloth and that the bucket of hot water was for bathing. Thankful for his persistence, I humbly took the bucket and washcloth.

Our group met in the hotel dining room for a complimentary breakfast. However, oddly enough, we were informed that the meal was only free to Indians. As unfair as that may have been, this was the case and not unusual.

Later, we arrived at the church where I was to preach. Outside of the small sanctuary was a large Hindu festival with loud music. The festivities made it nearly impossible to hear in the tiny church. It was like holding a service on Bourbon Street during Mardi Gras. The oppression of the enemy weighed heavily on these people.

Our next appointment was with native pastors from all over the country who were participating in the mission. The pastors all gave glowing reports on the mission. One reported five hundred baptisms, and another pastor's new membership had increased by nine hundred. These were the apexes of the reports, but each pastor had significant gains.

I encouraged them to seek and serve a big God, to dream big dreams, and to have big visions. I exhorted those who had had great success to encourage those who had had less.

Sadly, one of the local pastors coming to the meeting had slipped off a platform and been crushed by a train. In his hand, he had clutched the names of six hundred new believers. An offering was taken up for the family to help with their needs.

The following day, we trained twelve new church planters. These men were to go into villages to start up new churches. As the world changes and the West sends fewer missionaries overseas, it is imperative to raise up Nationals. Various churches agreed to sponsor each church planter for a year. Each was given $125 per month or 2,500 rupees, which is half of their salary. This is not much, but it was satisfactory. The church planters had no transportation. The Billy Gray Ministries (BGM) bought twelve new bicycles for their use.

It was quite challenging to teach these men how to share and answer questions. They were not well grounded in the Word, but they had a fervent love for the Lord and a desire to learn. I was not convinced that the training took full effect, but I did see some progress. If these men stay the course, they will win in the end.

The students were extremely complimentary and vowed that they had learned something. The seeds were planted, and I trusted the Holy Spirit to water and produce a bountiful harvest.

So much of humanity in India lives in a dark and hopeless world. Coming back to the hotel at midnight, I saw people squatting by the roadside, staring into the blackness. I wondered what they were thinking about. Was it hopes and dreams for a better tomorrow? Did they wonder if a hero would appear to rescue them? Or was it a futile prayer to a pagan god?

Moral decay was prevalent. Most marriages were still arranged, but in the larger cities, there was dating, along with premarital sex. Individual Christians were growing in Christ, and there was some increase in new believers. However, persecution of Christians and the prevalence of Hinduism stymied the growth.

As the sun began to make its presence known, the crows screeched with glee, expecting their daily banquet of leftovers tossed out by the restaurants. Day in and day out, this scenario repeated itself.

This was our last full day in Kakinada. I got up early and walked the stairs to the rooftop. The air was cool, and streets were still. I saw old people strolling around with seemingly no intent. The Muslims were fervently seeking Allah with chants on a loudspeaker. It was all vanity. God is the only hope. We will press on to share His hope.

A driver picked us up to take us to our new destination, Vijayawada, which was a four-hour drive away. The driver was frustrated about something, and the more agitated he got, the more recklessly he drove.

Once again, I was struggling to maintain a proper attitude. Our visions and goals were big, but there was little organization, and so much time was wasted. I could not fully grasp the concept of the vision. Our reports on numbers and money were conflicting.

I prayed, "Lord, if this is a lack of faith, please increase my faith. And, Lord, please help us get to our destination alive. Calm this driver's spirit."

Once the stressful car ride was over, I was relieved—and overjoyed to meet up with my longtime Indian friend, Lazarus, and his son. It was a breath of fresh air to see them. We retired for the night and planned to regroup the next day. The following morning, I had my first hot shower in five days.

We hired a taxi to take us to the orphanage. On previous days, the roads had been fairly well paved, and the cars had had air conditioning. But this day, it was like the India of old that I remembered. Treacherous roads that were narrow and winding with huge potholes, some as big as the footprint of a house.

We shared the road with people walking cattle, riding bicycles, and driving mopeds. Often, the road turned into something that a four-wheel-drive pickup truck dreamed of running through. This four-hour trip could easily have been made in under two hours had the roads been in decent condition. The jarring, thumping, and rocking was relentless and took its toll on my body.

Before going to the orphanage, we stopped at an ice-cream factory owned by Rafi, a dear friend of Lazarus's. Rafi and Lazarus had grown up together and attended the same school. Their affection for each other proved that they were kindred spirits. Their friendship reminded me of that of David and Jonathan.

Rafi was a kind, gentle, and loving man. He held church services in his plant for the entire village every Sunday. He was well known for his generosity. He had donated a brand-new sound system to Lazarus's church.

We made our way to Rafi's large, nice four-bedroom home. We accepted his invitation to stay for dinner and to spend the night. What a relief. I would be spared making that wretched four-hour drive back.

Before dinner, Lazarus and I went to visit the orphanage that he oversees and that the BGM supports financially. They had a huge, specially made sign at the entrance saying, "Welcome Dr. Billy Gray" (I have told them I am not a doctor, but they prefer to call me that anyway).

I was lovingly greeted by all the children and adults. They placed several handmade strings of fresh flowers around my neck. I was humbled and embarrassed by this lavish treatment like a king. Then I was greeted by John the Baptist, another beloved friend of mine, and his family. They presented me with more flowers. They were genuinely sweet people.

The children, all neatly dressed and clean and tidy, gathered around me and sang a song. They obediently followed instructions. There were twenty-two children, ages two to fourteen. I told the children how Jesus loves them and had a special plan for each one of them. They were enamored of me. They had never seen white skin before.

As we walked the orphanage grounds, all the children clung to me and touched some part of my body. I was grateful to the Lord that He had provided for these parentless little ones. All the children were healthy, learning about Jesus, and receiving a proper education; the orphanage was in good shape. Their primary need was continued funding, which the BGM will strive to provide as the Lord sees fit.

Before returning to Rafi's home for dinner and rest, BGM was able to give a financial gift to both Lazarus's and John the Baptist's ministries. This was only possible thanks to the Lord's provision and faithful contributors of the BGM. These God-fearing men were overjoyed with the gift. I trusted that they would use every dime to the glory of God.

Lazarus asked me to make one more stop at the home of a formerly Hindu couple, and I agreed. The husband and wife, who were now on fire for Jesus Christ, had two acres of land near Lazarus's church, and they donated these to him. I prayed over them and praised God for believers who were willing to make a sacrifice for the improvement of the body of Christ.

Finally, we reached Rafi's home. I was unusually tired. As I laid my head down, I could hear children in the next room watching cartoons. The temperature was below normal, there were no sheets on the bed, and I only had a baby-size blanket to cover up with. I slept in all my clothes, attempting to stay warm. This was not a lack of hospitality; it was the same in all the rooms.

Rafi and his family were delightful people. They served me as though I was their master and attempted to meet my every need. I enjoyed an edible breakfast of green tea, toast, and cheese. I was grateful for a bathroom break; however, there is no toilet paper there. The things we take for granted in the States are things they do not even consider.

After breakfast, we went to Lazarus's church to meet with twenty-five pastors. When we arrived, no one was there. I looked at my watch to check the time and discovered it was no longer working. Eventually, two men arrived and hurriedly set up chairs as though they were expecting a crowd. An hour later, twelve pastors arrived. I encouraged these men to live as though they could do all things through Jesus Christ who gives them the strength (Philippians 4:13). I told them to think big, because God is a big God, and our thoughts can never be bigger than His.

We were on a tight schedule and had to leave by 1:00 p.m. to reach Vijayawada. We left Lazarus's church and went back to the orphanage. The children were so happy to see me again and wanted to know when I would be coming back.

One little girl named Hannah kissed me on the cheek and looked me in the eye with her big, brown doe eyes. She told me she hoped I would come back soon. She reminded me of my daughter at that age. I felt so much love and warmth from the children that I hoped to endure this wretched travel to see them again someday, God willing.

Our next stop was to the home of a blind child whose parents were Hindu. I prayed for healing for the child and for spiritual insight for the parents. But the ride was exhausting and nerve racking. The price was supposed to be 2,000 rupees, but we were charged 4,400. The expense to repair my watch would be more than its cost. Maybe I could find another watch later. The soles of my only pair of shoes had come undone and were barely hanging on. And my sunglasses had been stepped on and crushed.

I was thankful finally to be back in a hotel room at the Raj Towers. There was peace and tranquility there. The following morning, I woke early, feeling rested. I waited for my bucket of hot water. It was like waiting for a baby to be delivered: you never knew when it would come.

I had two speaking engagements scheduled. My driver and interpreter for the day was a man named Elisha. One on one, Elisha's English was understandable, but when he was speaking English with other Indians, I could not understand him.

My first engagement was to a new church led by an inquisitive pastor. The message inspired very little reaction. Afterward, people wanted me to pray over them individually, but I told Elisha that I would do it collectively. This fell on deaf ears. So, one by one, I prayed for each individual and their needs.

Our next stop was to a village church. The village was primitive, and the car struggled to get down the narrow, alley-like streets. The structure itself was of blocks, with a tin roof. It had a doorway without a door and a dirt floor. The members were all tribal and worked in the fields during the day.

We were the first to arrive. Shortly, three children came with blankets and lay them out on the floor. The little building slowly filled up with an audience of people wearing an array of multicolored attire. Everyone had cleaned up after a long day of fieldwork and were wearing their finest.

The large pastor with the booming voice led the congregation in song, and the music belted out of the huge speakers. Sound systems are more of a priority than cement floors in Indian churches.

Elisha did a fine job of interpreting as I spoke. Again, people wanted me to pray over them individually. They requested prayer for sickness, withered hands, broken bones, and such. This was definitely India of old. I asked Elisha how much it would cost to cement the floor. He told me $400. The BGM paid to provide this church with a floor.

We stopped by Elisha's very nice home on the way back to the hotel. I met his lovely wife, who was a retired schoolteacher. And, much to my surprise, Elisha presented me with a new watch. I was caught off guard, embarrassed, and humbled. I received the watch with gratitude.

The next day, I left India and returned to Destin, Florida. I was utterly exhausted, totally spent, spiritually drained, and emotionally tapped out. This had been a challenging trip. Even so, I was grateful for the privilege to fellowship in Christ's sufferings and to spread the seed of His Word to a lost and dying world. I rejoiced in how He had blessed orphans, pastors, and churches through His provision of the ministry that He had placed under my care. I praised Him for the generosity of the Billy Gray Ministry partners and supporters.

Isaac (John the Baptist's father), his son, Samuel, Billy, and John the Baptist

Orphanage

CHAPTER 11
Belize

§

I FELL IN LOVE WITH Belize in the early 1970s. It presented itself to me as a land of opportunity, an untouched paradise, appealing to my frontier spirit. Deep down, my spirit longed for a change of venue. Something was missing in my life. I needed a new adventure.

The isle of Ambergris Key seemed to be the perfect place for this new escapade. The Barrier Reef was only about a mile out in the Caribbean; it was one of the best diving spots in the world, with emerald-green waters and fishing to die for.

This sparsely populated island only had one vehicle, a couple of mom-and-pop motels, and a half-built Catholic church. Most of the locals were of Indian descent. A few expatriates and European tourists made up the rest of the population.

My partner and I had purchased a large tract of land that had Caribbean frontage as well as bay frontage. The land, however, was tied up in an estate. After several years, my partner gave up. I was so tied emotionally to the property and the lifestyle that I soldiered on.

That is when God showed me how much He loved me by chastising me. I was accused of wrongdoing directly related to the property, which ultimately led to my arrest. From then on, my memories of Belize were of a land of broken dreams. My life had drastically changed between 1976 and 2014. No longer was I living in a large home. No longer did I have a practice with a prestigious law firm. Those days had been expunged and were replaced with an itinerant missionary life.

In 2014, an opportunity came up for me to go on a mission trip to Belize. I first rejected the idea because of all the bad memories, but the Holy Spirit kept urging me to go.

My grandson had expressed an interest in going on a mission trip with me for years. I renewed my effort of prayer when it occurred to me that this would be a perfect opportunity to take fourteen-year-old Caleb on his first mission trip.

English was the national language, eliminating the need for interpreters. We would be on the mainland, not on the key where all my previous experiences had been to dredge up unpleasant memories. A short flight would get us back to the United States if any illnesses occurred.

The first night at the opening rally, I was told we would be paired with the vice president from International Commission, Rick Pauly, and his wife, Juanita. I thought, *Good grief. I'm a loner. I don't need someone looking over my shoulder and holding me back.*

The Pauly's had tentative feelings regarding us as well. "We weren't sure what to expect when we were first told that we would be working with a gentleman named Billy Gray who had been on many International Commission trips and his young grandson, Caleb."

We may have been uncertain of each other at the start, but the Lord had certainly paired us together with a purpose. Rick Pauly sought me out and introduced himself. He was a soft-spoken gentleman; one hurdle cleared. His wife, Juanita, was a sweet, charming, and proficient lady. They both took to Caleb like a duck takes to water; this helped smooth my ruffled feathers. I knew we would be a great team. This couple is now a pair of my dearest friends.

The Pauly's later said, "After our first meeting at the church, we were excited to see what God was going to do in Belize. As the week went along, we witnessed a young man who was sure in his faith and was not afraid to share it. We saw him connect with several young boys around his age, and it was very exciting to see many of them accept Christ. We began increasingly appreciating knowing both Billy and Caleb and our growing friendship."

The rest of this adventure is told from the perspective of a fourteen-year-old boy on his first mission trip. Caleb shares how God used him on this mission despite his youth, anxiety, and awkwardness. This young man tells how he pressed forward in the face of setbacks and surprises. He expresses how life in Belize is drastically different from life in America. God can use anyone; He can use you too. You must be willing to submit and obey. Are you ready?

§

One day, Big Poppa said he had something important to discuss with me.

I wondered, "Uh oh, what did I do wrong?" I wasn't in trouble. Instead, he asked if I wanted to go on a mission trip with him to Belize. I said, "Yeah, I would love to go to Belize with you!"

Over the next few days, I had some concerns and doubts. Could I really do this mission stuff? Could I raise the money to go on the trip? My parents helped walk me through my doubts and questions. With God's help, I knew this was the right thing for me to do.

The day we left, we woke up at 3:00 a.m. and drove two hours to the airport, just to find out that our flight had been canceled. The next flight wasn't until the following day at the same time. So we drove back the two hours and waited for the next morning. I started thinking, *Are we even going to do this?*

The next morning, we repeated the same early schedule. This time our flight was on time, but we had to take an extra flight through Texas. We finally arrived in Belize, and I immediately noticed the strange, tropical surroundings. I am from Florida, but this place has different stuff. Coconut trees everywhere, banana plants, and huge lizards called wishing willy's that grow up to three feet long.

We waited in the airport for an hour for our ride to take us to the hotel, but no one ever showed up. Big Poppa had to get us a taxi. Our driver's name was, George, and so far, he was the highlight of the day. He was happy to tell us all about Belize. I told him that I wanted to see the Mayan ruins. He gave us his card and told us to call him when we were ready to take a tour, promising he would take care of us.

That night, the mission teams met at the main church. We were then teamed up into smaller groups of four. Our group consisted of me, Big Poppa, and the Pauly's. Like Big Poppa, the Pauly's were seasoned warriors of God. Our group was stationed at the main church, where we met Pastor Ralph.

The next morning was Sunday; Big Poppa preached at our assigned church. He's a very good storyteller, and all the people sat on the edges of their seats, listening to his every word. At the conclusion of Big Poppa's sermon, Pastor Ralph was noticeably amazed by his skills and said, "There wasn't a dry eye left in the church."

After that, we went to Sunday school. I was in a group with other teens, while Big Poppa was with the adults. One of the boys read a passage from the Bible. I couldn't understand what he was reading, though I could hear some English words mixed in. I must have looked confused, because the teacher stopped the boy and told him to read in English. Another teen, Glen, explained to me that the boy had been reading in Creole, which is a mixture of French and English words that the Belizeans speak. No wonder I couldn't understand the words. Glen and I quickly became friends. He was the son of the youth pastor, Juan, and the grandson of Pastor Ralph.

After lunch, our team, along with Glen, went door to door to witness to people in the neighborhood. The houses were compact and crammed together. Most of them were made out of clay, bricks, and cinderblocks. Almost all had fences around the entire yard, with a Beware of Dog sign. Most people had pit bulls. People are very suspicious and cautious due to the bad crime rate in Belize. And Belize is a country below sea level, so many of the homes had aboveground septic tanks. Gross! They also put their dead in aboveground tombs.

As we went door to door, some people would not talk to us, some people listened to us and smiled, and others invited us into their homes. One lady's home was small and cluttered with all sorts of clothes, papers, and books. After moving a pile of clothes, she invited us to sit on her old sofa. The springs were visibly poking out and jabbing into my leg. It was hot and stuffy in there; the only air movement came from the open door. We were all dripping wet with sweat after being there for a short time. I don't know how she stood that heat.

Big Poppa asked her if Jesus was her Lord and Savior. She started telling us that God had abandoned her and didn't love her. In the saddest way ever, she told us how her younger brother, a well-known soccer player, had been murdered. Tears ran down her face. Then she got angry. "How could a loving God allow this to happen to my brother? He was so kind and good!" she cried.

Big Poppa reminded her that God's love is perfect. His Only Son was also murdered to save us from our sins. He allowed that because He loves us. Right then, she rededicated her life to Jesus.

Just then, her fourteen-year-old son, Marco, walked into the house. Big Poppa asked him if he was a Christian. He said that he wasn't. Big Poppa turned to me and said, "Caleb, tell Marco about Jesus."

I showed Marco the pictures on the EvangeCube. I told him how God is our Creator and He sent Jesus to save us from our sins so we could live with Him in heaven. Marco asked Jesus into his heart! We went to more houses, and nine more people accepted Jesus that day!

As we were heading back to Glen's, two neighborhood boys ran up to me, holding a two-foot-long baby crocodile they had caught in the creek behind their house. They were trying to convince me to buy it from them and to take it back to America with me as a souvenir. "I don't need a crocodile. Besides, how would I get it home?"

They said, "In your suitcase."

The next day, we met up with Glen again. He brought me a coconut from his yard and showed me how to open it, and then we drank the milk right out of it. The day before, we had knocked down a coconut from a tree at my hotel, but when I had tasted it, it was disgusting. So Glen had promised to bring me a good one.

While hanging out with Glen, I asked him if he had any pets. He said, "I once caught a lizard and kept it for a while, but then I let it go." He paused, looked down at the ground, and then said, "We had a dog once, but one day, we came home from church and found him strung up in a tree, hanging from a rope, with a sign around his neck that said, 'You are bad owners and drove me to suicide.'"

Wow! I didn't really know what to say to that. So I changed the subject and asked him if he had any siblings. He said, "Yes, I have two." Again, he paused, looked down at the ground and said, "Only one is left, though. My older brother was kidnapped a few months ago. The kidnappers sent us a video of his torture and execution. They strangled him, cut him up a lot, shot him in the thumb, and then shot him in the back of the head, killing him. They caught the guys who killed my brother, and now they're in jail."

Again, I didn't know what to say. I kind of thought that he was making this stuff up to "impress" me. But his dad was standing right there, listening to the entire conversation, and never once objected to what Glen was saying.

Glen's dad told me that they had just moved to this neighborhood. They had had to leave their other home because the gang violence around it was so bad. One night, as the family had been eating supper, a gang shot up their house, thinking it was the home of a rival gang member.

Belize is a different world from the one I'm used to. We don't have a clue how blessed we are in America. These people have to worry all the time about crime and violence. Almost everyone I met there had lost someone to murder.

The next day, we gained two more fourteen-year-old boys for our evangelizing group. Glen and I had witnessed to them the day before, and this day, they met up with us to witness to other people. We continued witnessing door to door in the neighborhoods. We heard many sad stories, made many new friends, and witnessed many people ask Jesus into their hearts.

Each night at the church service, more and more neighborhood people showed up. It was cool seeing God work in so many lives.

One day, our group went to a soup kitchen where they fed the homeless. Let me just say, this place was a real experience. When I first got there, I saw an old-looking mother cradling her teenage daughter like a newborn baby. Every once in a while, the daughter would let out a blood-curdling scream. This freaked me out. I'd never seen or heard anything like this.

Then, a young boy around ten years old came up to me and asked me for my shoes. I told him these were the only shoes I had and that I couldn't give them away. He then asked me for some money. I told him I didn't have any to give away. He looked down at my pants and saw my wallet in my pocket and said, "Isn't that your wallet? Give me some money."

The next day was a free day for us. Big Poppa, the Pauly's, and I decided to stick together and see some sights. We called up our man, George, to escort us around. He first took us to the beautiful Mayan ruins and had his friend give us a very informative tour. Then we went into the rain forest, where we got to feed monkeys. This was an awesome experience! I got to hold a monkey and a crocodile.

I saw the most vibrant, lime-green snake I'd ever seen. I also saw huge ants as big as cockroaches, working together to bring stuff into their mound. We had the best rice and fried chicken I'd ever eaten in my life at a little shack in the middle of the rain forest.

When we got back to our hotel room, Big Poppa said I needed to be prepared to share my testimony in front of the church. I was so nervous about this. I sat down and wrote out what I wanted to say, and then I practiced it over and over again out loud in front of Big Poppa.

Before I knew it, Glen's dad was waiting outside to take us to the church. We arrived at the night service, and the congregation had doubled since our first one. We sang lots of songs, and then my turn to speak came up. I took my piece of paper and went to the pulpit. I was so nervous and embarrassed that even though I had memorized what I was going to say, I couldn't keep my eyes off of my paper. I ended up reading the entire thing.

I read: "I grew up in a Christian home, where my parents did not force me to love the Lord. They did tell me about Him and how Jesus died on the cross to save me from my sins.

"One day when I was talking to them, I saw that they had something that I didn't have, something that made them a lot happier, and I wanted to have that same something too. I realized that that something was Jesus Christ.

"That day, I asked a lot of questions about Jesus. I learned that Romans 3:23 tells us we are all sinners and John 3:16 tells us God loved us so much, He gave His Son to die on the cross to save us from our sins. I admitted that I was a sinner, believed Jesus saved me from my sins, and I committed my life to Him.

"Psalm 3:14 says, 'Free me from the trap that is set before me, for Jesus is my refuge.' I like this verse because whenever I sin, I know He will save me from the sin trap, that He still loves me, and that I always have a home in heaven because He is my refuge.

"After that, I wanted to tell other people about Jesus Christ. It has been a great joy serving here and sharing Jesus with the people of Belize. If you don't know that Jesus is your Savior, I hope you will ask Him into your life so you can have peace and a home in heaven."

After all the speaking was done, Glen and another adult came up to me separately and said, "Nice speech." They did not say this in a condescending or rude manner; they were sincere.

In my head, I laughed, thinking, *I guess it was more like a speech than a story.* It's funny, because when I think about that moment, it makes me grin to remember how awkward I was. But that's OK. The important thing is that I did it and didn't let fear scare me off.

We had one last service the next morning. Big Poppa gave an even better sermon than the first one. Many people crowded around him afterward to speak with him and thank him for his wonderful sermons.

We said our final good-byes. Some people exchanged small gifts. The Pauly's gave me a Belize mug to remember them and our trip by, which I still have and cherish. When I look at the mug, I remember all that I learned from Belize and the people I met there.

After we got home, Big Poppa sent me a note saying,

Master Caleb,

It was a delight to see you embolden with the Holy Spirit and share your faith with complete strangers, standing before a congregation and telling them how Jesus came into your life. You may think your Big Poppa is a bold witness and a good preacher, but when I was fourteen, I would not have had the courage to do what you did. You got a head start on me, and one day as I look down from heaven, I'll nudge St. Peter and say, "That's my grandson, sharing Jesus with others."

You da' man!

When you least expect it, God may call you on a mission trip. It doesn't matter how young or old you are or if you are awkward or polished. All that matters is that you obey His call. All sorts of challenges will pop up causing you to doubt, but you have to cling to Him.

This was a great experience that I'm so thankful was given to me, and I'm glad I accepted. If you are called, you should go. God will take care of you.

Mr. and Mrs. Pauly, Billy Gray, and Caleb Plantholt

Caleb with a monkey

CHAPTER 12
Tanzania

§

THE MEMPHIS-TO-TANZANIA FLIGHT TOOK FIFTY-TWO hours. I traveled with a group of thirty-five people; most of the team was from California, Texas, or Oklahoma, with a few from Florida, Colorado, or Arizona.

After arriving in Nairobi, we had a ten-hour bus ride to Arusha. The traveling was strenuous. The open windows allowed dust into the bus, which irritated my lungs and caused me to develop a nasty cough that later turned into pneumonia.

God's grace and strength allowed me to serve all but one day on this mission trip. It was a day of great honor that I wish I had been able to attend. But I will tell that story later.

The main language in Tanzania is Swahili; however, most of the people in the hotels spoke English very well. I follow the TINA rule while traveling overseas: "This is not America." The objective is to share how Christ has changed our lives instead of trying to westernize people. Half of the Tanzanians are Christian; 40 percent are Muslim. The two groups coexist peaceably together.

Tanzania had become a popular destination for those interested in photo safaris and less popular for game hunting. In the hotel in Arusha, we saw many people seeking safari adventures. I had the privilege of attending one of these safaris, but I was not impressed. Honestly, I saw more animals in closer range at Busch Gardens, in Tampa, Florida than I did in Africa.

The following day, we visited the village of Olmringiringa. We were immediately greeted by an African community filled with love and friendliness. The villagers belong to the tribe of Maasai, known as the hospitable tribe. Their love and friendliness toward their fellow country-men also extended to us outsiders. This tribe did not have tribal disputes like other tribes in Kenya.

Our time in this village was spent visiting families in their homes. Pastor Samuel, the local Christian pastor in the village, accompanied us.

Most of the villagers were farmers, growing cabbage, sugarcane, and coffee, selling the fruits of their harvest at market. The gross family income was approximately $200 a year. The villagers had no electricity or running water within their homes. The twenty-first century had not spoiled these people. Without electricity, there were no television or handheld devices.

One way the Tanzanians showed their generosity was through sharing meals. Each day, I ate at Pastor Samuel's home for lunch. Afterward, we would recline and rest, as is the custom. I was informed that it would be disrespectful not to eat all that was served to me. Since I was not certain of what exactly they were eating, I told them that I did not eat meat. I mainly feasted on bananas, rice, hard-boiled eggs, and melons.

At first, I was shocked by the local eating habits, but I quickly grew to enjoy their intimate fellowship. Five gracious women served ten men sitting at a table. After serving us, the ladies would retire under a shade tree, where they would relax, talk, and knit. None of that was surprising or unusual; what was, was when the grown men would stick their hands into my bowl of food, take out a handful of *my* food, and put it into their own bowls. That caught me off guard. But this was perfectly acceptable and normal for them. As I said before, I grew to enjoy this, though I do not plan on making it a tradition at my own dinner table.

The young people were very curious about the United States. They knew America was big and strong, but that was the extent of their knowledge. They asked a lot of questions: "Are all Americans Christians? Do Americans just have one wife?" They were amazed that I had my own car and that I drove myself. No one in the village owned a car. They seldom saw any, as most had never been to the big city of Arusha where there are many cars.

Pastor David Duvall, from Northbay Baptist Church in Niceville, Florida, had presented me with a new digital camera just before I departed for Africa. This gave me the opportunity to take photos of the children. They were thrilled and delighted to see photos of themselves, for they had never seen such a thing.

One young man I met was building a one-room house. He was in his early twenties and seemed to be in a hurry to finish. I asked him why he was rushing. "When I complete my house, then I can choose a girl from our village and make her my wife," he explained. "After that, I'm going to save my money and buy a car." I believed this young man would persevere and make his dreams come true.

Before church began, I could hear the choir director with his falsetto voice leading the choir, practicing for the upcoming service. Most songs sounded the same to me, but each one was perfectly in tune with the rich rhythm of the African vibe. Their diligence paid off, because they always successfully worked the congregation up into a fevered pitch with shouts of joy and praises to God. The people were then ready to receive the Gospel as a desert pilgrim receives water. There were always new converts at the end of each service.

Within the village, each man had several wives. Pastor Samuel told me that his grandfather had seven. The men who became Christians were allowed to keep all their wives since Christianity would not want them to abandon a responsibility they had incurred before their conversion.

The chief of the village was an unbeliever. He was a tall and stately man. He wore a brilliant blue and vibrant red cloak and carried a tall, Moses-like staff. He and I sat on tiny stools in an open field under the blazing-hot sun. I shared with him how Christ had changed my life; he listened intently. Pastor Samuel aided the encounter by translating verses from his Swahili Bible.

The chief's heart was transformed, and as I was leaving, he said, "May *our* God bless you." He then reached out and grabbed my shoulder and said, "Please come back tomorrow. I will have a special ceremony for you."

As I was on my way to take my ride back to the hotel, Pastor Samuel showed me a vacant lot next to his house. He said, "Brother Billy, we would like to invite you to come and live with us. I own the lot next to my house. We will build you a house, teach you our language, and you can live the rest of your life in our peaceful village."

I was struck by the magnitude and the generosity of his offer. But I politely declined, saying, "Pastor Samuel, that is such a generous offer. It would be an honor and a privilege to live among such a loving community of people. But I have two children and three grandchildren back in America. I'm not ready to move so far away from them on a permanent basis." He accepted my excuse and said he understood.

As we traveled back to our hotel, I sat in the back of a three-row van. The dust was so thick that I could not see the driver. Several times, the van got stuck in the dust like vehicles get stuck in the sand at the beach. The roads were horrible, with craters large enough to swallow an elephant.

Breathing the dust worsened my cough considerably. That night, my body finally reached its limit. I spent the night racked with pain, incessantly coughing, burning up one minute and then drenched with sweat and freezing the next.

The next morning, I had intended to visit the chief and to participate in the ceremony he had prepared for me, but I was unable to get out of bed. As the hours went on, my cough continued to worsen; breathing became a chore.

The ceremony was held despite my absence. Pastor Samuel came back later that night to check on me. He presented me with a scepter and a ceremonial robe from the chief. Pastor Samuel said, "You are the only person in history ever to be made an honorary tribal chief by the Olmringiringa tribe. This is the greatest honor the chief could ever bestow upon you." I was grieved that I had missed the ceremony; I was humbled and honored by the recognition.

Shortly before heading back to the States, our mission team went to a wild-game restaurant in Nairobi. The menu included veal, beef, and chicken, along with exotic wild-game choices. I went out on a limb and decided to try ostrich, crocodile, and camel. The ostrich and crocodile were bearable; the camel was horrible—tough as leather and bitter. The waiters came around with the meat on a big stick, sliced it, and put whatever we wanted onto our plates. I enjoyed the ice cream the most.

If I had been a man without a family, I might have seriously considered Pastor Samuel's offer. There was something intriguing about a peaceful village that was unencumbered by the twenty-first century's enticements. It seemed as though living such an unpretentious life would eliminate the distractions, allowing for more focus on Christ. The villagers lived a modest life, though it was far from easy.

You may say, "Well, you could move there and still visit your family." If I did make that move, I would not make enough money to be able to visit my family. Also, I firmly believe God has put me where He has put me for a reason.

Could I give up the American lifestyle and the luxuries of my life for God? By His strength and according to His will, I could and I would. God has called all of us to serve Him and to witness His love and truth. Some are called to live out their lives in a tiny village in Africa, some are called to be stay-at-home moms, and some are called to go to a variety of places. We are *all* called. We must all be obedient to His call.

Where is your call? Are you obeying Him?

The chief and Billy Gray

Tanzanian children

CHAPTER 13

Haiti

§

I WAS STUNNED AS I watched the nightly news. On January 12, 2010, a reporter announced that a 7.0-magnitude earthquake had caused a mass catastrophe in Haiti, sixteen miles west of Port-au-Prince, the capital. Significant damage or total destruction occurred to the presidential palace, Port-au-Prince Cathedral, the National Assembly building, jails, banks, mortuaries, homes, and much more. More than thirteen hundred schools and fifty health-care facilities had been destroyed. Many orphanages had been devastated. Major roads were blocked. Rescue efforts were hampered due to damage to communication systems. Air, land, and sea transports were immobile. Aftershocks continued. The people were desperately frightened.

Haiti has been known as the poorest country in the Western Hemisphere. The majority of the people live in poorly constructed houses made out of any material found in the area: planks of wood, large pieces of plastic, sheets of metal, cloth, plastic, or tarps. Homes have no running water, sewage, or electricity. I wondered how a country already living in such dire straits would survive such an event. Only the God of heaven could know.

Weeks later, more than fifty-two aftershocks measuring on the Richter scale at 4.5 or greater were recorded. This devastation had affected 3 million people. The death toll was reported at 130,000.

Many people slept on the streets, in cars, or makeshift shanty towns because their homes were destroyed or they feared structures falling in on them. There was fuel shortage and potable-water deficiency.

Thousands of bodies were scattered all over the place. So many dead; mortuaries had been demolished. Smells of decomposing bodies buried in the unmoved rubble lingered in the air. It was pure madness. As time went on, the dead bodies increased. Some neighborhoods came together, singing songs at night to relieve the oppression. Men worked together to act as security against the looters and acts of violence. Women coordinated and helped with food preparation and distribution as well as hygiene.

Displaced citizens were being intimidated by lawbreakers. Sexual, domestic, and gang violence went on the rise. Rapes of Haitian women and girls living in camps drastically increased.

As the Southeastern side of the United States was blanketed with unusually cold weather and utility bills rose, I gave praise to God for my abundant blessings. I had a warm home, clothes to wear, plenty to eat, and good drinking water.

Over three million Haitians were in great need of pure drinking water. Soon after the earthquake, I sent out a plea to the Billy Gray Ministries partners to help raise money for water filters. The goal was to send two thirty-pound water filters into remote areas of Haiti. Within a week, the faithful BGM partners generously gave, and the request was made possible.

Five weeks after the earthquake, I left for Haiti. At the request of the Florida Baptist Children's Home, I was asked to help develop plans and facilities for 250 orphans.

Going to Haiti was like Jesus's return. No one knew what to expect, not even Ron Gunter, the leader of this mission. Fifteen other people from various areas across the United States also accepted this call to help the orphans in Haiti. We all met Ron at the Miami airport, and from there, we flew to Santiago, Dominican Republic.

As we flew in, I could see jagged mountains with fertile valleys interspersed. The Dominican Republic and Haiti share one island but two very different countries. The Dominican Republic is a popular tourist destination that appears to be like paradise, with breathtaking landscapes and luxurious hotels. Several million tourists vacation there each year.

So, one country on this island, is a popular vacation spot; the other was now a land of hopeless despair. The literacy rate in the Dominican Republic is 90 percent, whereas only 50 percent of Haitians could read. The Dominican Republic had good roads throughout, while the Haitian roads were atrocious, with weak infrastructure hampering quick delivery of aid during any emergency situation. The Dominican Republic had running water, electricity, and sewer systems; much of Haiti did not. It was a startling contrast.

The first night, we stayed in a lavish hotel in Santiago. Trying to rest and sleep was useless, because we had arrived during carnival time. The festivities were loud, the music was booming, and the crowds were rowdy.

The next day after breakfast, we departed for a three-hour bus ride to the Haitian border. The long trip gave us plenty of time to get better acquainted with one another and to form a cohesive group. We all had two things in common: we loved the Lord first and foremost, and we desired to go wherever He called us to go.

We drove along the Cordillera Septentrional mountain range and entered Haiti. Border patrol, with armed guards, insisted we take no pictures. The visual differences between the two countries was shocking. To say Haiti looked like a cesspool would have been an understatement.

During our long drive, we did not see any structural or geographical damage. What we did see was far worse: damaged lives. The windows to their souls showed hopelessness.

Our bus stopped because it could go no further. With luggage in hand, we walked the distance of two football fields, negotiating potholes filled with garbage. The road was difficult just to walk on and impossible to drive on.

The buildings were poorly built. The people were incredibly poor. In the distance, I saw Haitians dressed in white gowns, having a lively baptismal ceremony in the river, while we were surrounded by beggars besieging us. This was surreal.

Upon reaching our hotel, I climbed up steep, uneven stairs with my luggage to the third floor. I was blown away at how nice my room was compared to what I had just seen outside. The room was relatively clean, had screens on the windows, and an oscillating fan that worked when the electricity worked.

I was relieved to discover that the orphanage was in walking distance from the hotel. It was large and spread out. It was ten years old, schooled six hundred children, and fed them lunch daily. It served seventeen thousand meals each month, also feeding other children from town. Often, this was their only meal. Astonishingly, the accomplished and courteous staff could count the origin of all but three of these children.

The orphanage was currently in the process of building a clinic and a hospital. People from the States came every week, many staying for months, to help with this incredible operation. American Christians could give praise to God, knowing that so many faithful believers made this trek to serve their fellow man and God.

Our mission was to work with the children from Port-au-Prince who had lost their parents or who had been abandoned. I was overcome by the never-ending cries. Infants cried as a loving volunteer cuddled them, holding the babes on their chests while lying on a bed covered by a mosquito net.

Baby had been fed and was clean. All of his or her essential needs were met but one: Mother. Baby instinctively knew this was not Mother. Love, food, and shelter alone would never replace her, but the baby would never know his or her mother. They would grieve in their own way, at their own pace. But in time, they would learn how much they were truly loved by a large, extended family.

Then my eyes were accosted by the injustice of all of this: little babies with heads as big as basketballs and bodies as tiny as a Chihuahua's. There were children forever paralyzed and dependent upon someone for their every need, from now until God called them home. Wheelchairs, walkers, and crutches were all too plentiful. Children were bedridden with severed arms or legs or broken bones. These were things I might have expected to see in the elderly, not the young.

I began my first full day at the orphanage having a devotion with children on the playground. The children sat quietly and were well disciplined.

They had big, beautiful, infectious smiles with pearly-white teeth. The children who had lived in the orphanage for some time spoke English very well.

After the devotion, I was given the job of separating and sorting thousands of pairs of donated shoes by size and condition. Some of the shoes in the bins were good, some bad, and others were not worthy of letting a dog chew them. This was an overwhelming and physically demanding task. Exhausted that night, my head could barely wait to hit the pillow.

The following morning, I reflected on the children, staff, volunteers, and townspeople I had seen or met. Hope sprang eternal for some, but not most. Some were starving, many were fearful, others were in pain. Some desperately gathered at the border, ready to beg or sell their souls for a single moment of a full stomach, peace, or being free from pain. It all seemed so futile until God's hand was revealed.

At the orphanage, children were clothed, educated, taught manners, and learned to show respect. These children were pointed toward the Cross, the Bread of Life, the Prince of Peace, the Provider, and the Living Water.

My task, for the next day, was to sort clothes and shoes. It was miserably hot, and the mosquitos were abundant. I spent more time swatting mosquitos than actually sorting.

Later, I walked the campus and had the privilege of interacting with the children. I met two young ladies from New York who had taken their vacation time to serve in Haiti. While at home, these young ladies had a ministry with inner-city kids. They proved to be skillful organizers and played water-game activities with the children. The children were delighted and absolutely loved the games. Laughter filled my ears, and joy swelled my heart.

These two young ladies spent most of their time loving on and caring for the special-needs children. They possessed the tender and gentle touch these little ones needed. They required constant, 24/7 care, and their little lives revolved around eating, sleeping, and crying. Some had cerebral palsy; others had degenerative diseases. One child was the size of a six-month-old, yet he was ten years old. Another child had been found abandoned in a room with thirty-six other babies; some of them had been alive while others lay dead. It required very special people, filled with the love and compassion of Jesus, to be able to pour themselves out into the lives of these needy children.

Afterward, I met, Addie, an eleven-year-old girl who had lived in the orphanage since the age of two. She wore her royal-blue school uniform with pride. She had a smile that radiated and eyes that sparkled. Her older brother also lived at the home. She told me she had two sisters; one lived in New York, but of the other sister she did not know the whereabouts. Her mother was deceased, and she knew nothing of her father. Addie told me she loved it at the orphanage and that she was very happy and well cared for. Her bright countenance proved this statement to be true.

Next, I met Astrid, a twelve-year-old who had lost her right arm and sustained a broken leg during the earthquake. She sat in her wheelchair with her leg propped up, sharing a smile that lit up the room. She told me that when the lights went out at night, her mind shifted to dark and frightening places. She could still clearly see the carnage of her dead brothers and sisters and her daddy lying helplessly in a ditch as she begged and screamed for someone to help him. The help had never come.

She could remember the voices of the frantic doctors and nurses who had amputated her arm. She recalled that on the table next to her had been a boy having his leg amputated. She could still hear the sounds of the pounding hammer and the grinding saw. The nights for her were long and horrifying, but light comes with the rising sun, and her hope and peace was refreshed.

Then I met Serge, a twenty-four-year old man. He had lost his right leg when the earthquake brought his house crashing down upon him. He was a sole survivor: he had also lost his mother, father, seven sisters, and four brothers. Even at his advanced age, the orphanage dutifully took him in, because he had no family and no education.

One of the most helpful people I met was eighteen-year-old Johnson. He was my dutiful interpreter and the first resident in the house. He was a talented young man who aspired to stay at the orphanage as an employee.

My evening concluded with a time of witnessing to a group of four-teen-to-eighteen-year-old boys. Johnson accompanied me and translated as I presented the Gospel through the EvangeCube. The boys were still and attentive to my every word. Several boys prayed the sinner's prayer. There was a thirst for God among the group. I continued to meet with them each night. By the end of my trip, I was confident that each of those boys knew Jesus as his personal Savior.

At the conclusion of each day, it was my responsibility to escort the women from the orphanage to the hotel. It was too dangerous for the ladies to walk alone.

The next day, I woke up early, feeling physically exhausted but filled with the Spirit to move forward. We visited a village, distributing clothes to the exceptionally poor. It was an enjoyable project and nice to see the gratitude of the receivers.

Some of the children in the village we recognized from the school. At school, the children wore nice uniforms, but in the village, they were either naked or poorly dressed. These were children who lived right outside the walls of the orphanage but did not have the advantages of living in it or its free lunches.

We returned to the orphanage. Suddenly, we heard a low rumble, a crumble, a tumble, and a loud crashing sound that could be heard over the entire campus. Children were in hysterics, frightened like horses spooked by lightning. Mass chaos ensued. Children ran out of the school, the cafeteria, and the chapel, grabbing their possessions. Some were knocked to the ground; others were trampled underfoot. All were seeking higher ground, a safe haven. Their delicate nerves were strewn asunder. In their minds, their peaceful cohabitation had been shattered due to their recent trauma.

An eight-foot-high concrete wall surrounding the property had collapsed. Just outside it, workers had been digging footings for the new hospital but had dug too close to the wall, causing 150 feet of it to collapse. It was a miracle the fifteen workers had just taken a lunch break. Praise God, no one was hurt.

It was a long night of calming the anxieties of these fragile children, reassuring them that it had not been an earthquake and that they were safe. Tomorrow would bring new beginnings. Our God is a god of love, compassion, and second chances. I praised Him in the arms of Jesus.

The next day, we departed Haiti to return home. It was a free-border day, which meant that thousands of people were trying to cross the border to go to the Dominican Republic side.

The previous day, Ron had taken our passports and exit slips to get preclearance so we could avoid the crowds. If anything had happened to those documents or to Ron, we would have been stuck in Haiti for a long time. We put our faith in our Protector and Provider.

The morning was gray, with a light rain and a gentle breeze. The rain from the previous night had turned the streets into thick mud. We waded our way through ankle-deep mud and crawled into the back of a truck covered with a leaky tarp. As we traveled toward the border, I saw a mass of humanity like I had never seen before. People carried sacks of flour, pushed carts, and rode motor scooters, all while watching out for pickpockets. Thankfully, Ron's preclearance efforts had worked, and we were able to cross the border without any delay.

Hardships have a place in believer's lives because "our light and momentary troubles are achieving for us an eternal glory that far outweighs them all" (2 Corinthians 4:17). As we walk through trials, they never seem light and momentary, but in comparison to eternity, they certainly are minuscule. During such difficult times, we must redirect our focus from fear to faithfulness. Then we will be strengthened by His power to move forward.

God pours out His strength and power into our souls right on time. Without His strength and power, I could not have endured this mission. I pray that God will redirect the Haitian believers' hearts away from fear and toward faithfulness. Also, that their love and trust in Christ will be contagious in a lost and dark country.

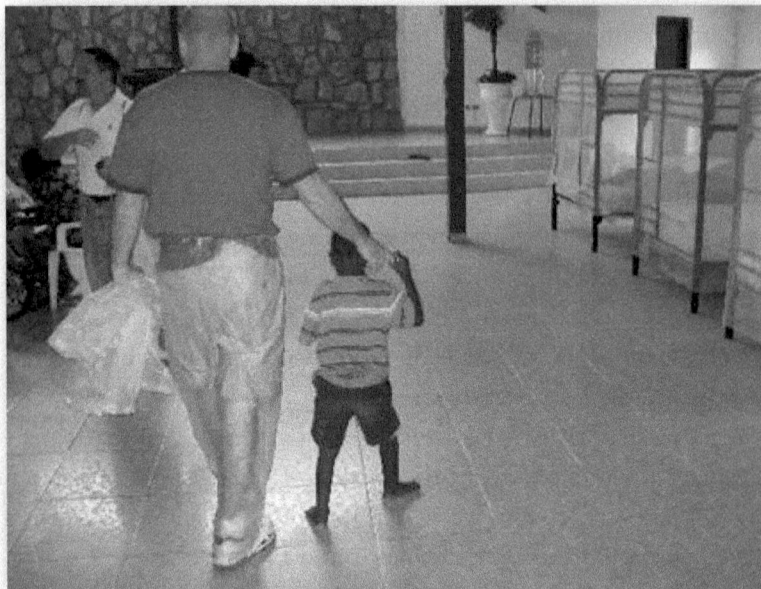

Billy's little helper

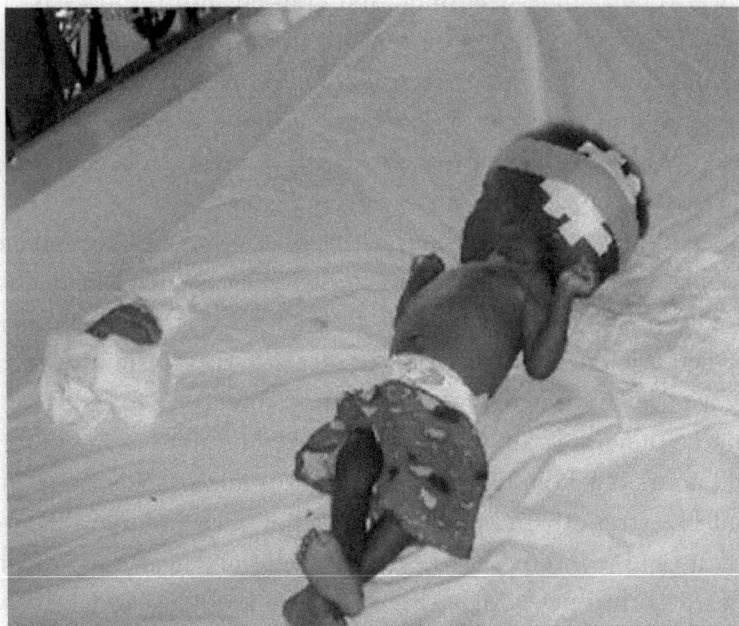

Orphan with an abnormally large head

CHAPTER 14
India: Particular Events

§

IT IS DIFFICULT NOT TO be loquacious while talking about India. I have traveled there twenty times, to various cities and to countless villages. There are sundry stories to tell and pictures to paint. This chapter consists of a medley of India stories from different areas and different times.

India is a restless place. Cars whiz by all night; horns honk, dogs bark. It is like an itch that cannot be satisfied or a foreign object in the eye that cannot be dispelled.

India is a place where you can actually see the lame walk, witness vision restored to the blind, and observe people being set free from demon possession.

India is a country of caste systems, where the lowest of the lowest are cast out and ignored. It is a country where prearranged marriages still exist. India is a country of diverse lifestyles, from people living in modern homes to small villages to tribal communities, all the way down to children living in dumps.

India is a place where parents abandon their children, leaving them to fend for themselves because they cannot afford to feed another hungry mouth. Some parents break their child's legs to gain more sympathy when begging.

India's main roads are horrendous. The village roads are dirt or mud, depending on the weather. The government is hostile toward missionaries, and many Christians are persecuted for their beliefs. Hinduism, a religion in which people believe in reincarnation and pray to a variety of gods, reigns in India.

Much of India is a dark and hopeless place that desperately needs the Light of Hope. Upon entering India, I quickly gained insight into how very different this world was from the life I lived in the States.

The Delhi train station was filthy and unkempt. The ancient engines were still powered by coal. The train station was as busy as the Atlanta airport during the holiday season. Starving dogs walked the tracks, scouring them for food and looking as though they hoped to be hit by a train. Parentless children, as young as two years old, crawled or walked on the disgusting floor. They begged for food or grabbed whatever they could get their grimy little hands around. Many of these children die from malnutrition.

Our group waded through hordes of people while we carried our luggage. Then we loaded onto a bus with seats so tiny, my knees nearly touched my chin. The train station employees tossed our luggage on top of the roof, tying it down with ropes. And so, the mission began.

One evening, in a small village outside of Guntur, my thoughts were, *Oh God, why am I here?* Sick with a lung infection and a skyrocketing fever, I was exhausted, wearied, and drained. However, this mission had been planned for and bathed in prayers for two years. The village was totally committed to the crusade and eager for our arrival. So I pulled myself out of the sickbed to preach.

John the Baptist and Lazarus, my two trusty aides, picked me up for the one-hour drive. Several locals accompanied us in the van. It was pouring down rain on this velvety black night, and I soon discovered that my window only rolled up halfway. The windshield wipers did not work, causing Lazarus to continually wipe the window with his hand as he drove. No one was exactly sure where the village was. We just kept driving, lost and uncertain.

The rain came down harder. I was soaking wet, shivering, constantly coughing, and growing weaker. Death would have been a welcome relief. My temperature was rising, and I was racked with pain. Silently, I cried to the Lord, "Please, let them quit and take me back to the hotel."

After three hours of driving, the chatty Indian passengers grew quiet and still. A sense of pessimism permeated the air. After a long stint of silence, Lazarus informed me that we were finally on the right road. Once again, the group grew optimistic, and the chattiness returned.

The rain was relentless. Looking out of my window, I could see the tires were sinking into the mud up to the hubcaps. We slowly continued on in what we believed was the right direction.

The night was so dark and the rain was so heavy that we could only see a watery blob of a view where the headlights shined. Far in the distance, we saw a light swinging back and forth. The chatter in the van increased with obvious fear. We continued to drive toward the light, not knowing what we would find. Finally, we were able to make out a man frantically swinging a lantern and signaling for us to stop.

The lantern man warned us that the road had given way to the torrential rain, sustaining a six-foot hole. This harbinger of light had saved our lives. There was no way we would have seen the hole in time to avoid falling in.

Lantern man placed two planks of wood across the hole for us to walk across. We all exited the vehicle, waded our way through thick, ankle-deep mud, and nimbly crossed the planks. On the other side of the chasm stood sixty villagers in two straight lines. Each person was holding a lantern, making a lighted path for us up to the church door about fifty yards away.

The church was jam-packed and jelly tight, standing room only. The three-hour delay had not deterred the villagers from waiting on what they had come to hear.

For at least an hour we stood, clapping and singing, summoning the Holy Spirit. With the atmosphere ripe and full of the Spirit, I rose to speak. As I began to preach a message of salvation, and mercy, God gave me a boost of adrenalin. My fever lifted, my cough subsided, and my voice was strong. The presence of the Spirit moved over the congregation like a shadow on a sunny day. The response was tremendous; the altar was full of hundreds of people claiming Jesus as their Lord and Savior, confessing sins, and reconciling broken relationships. God had truly outdone Himself.

Wherever He leads, I will go. This is why I'm here, I thought. *Thank you, Lord, for not letting me miss this amazing moment.* The satisfaction of this gift far outweighed the hardship of getting to this point.

Another trip, taken shortly after the 9/11 terrorist attacks, took me to Tirupati, India. The headlines in the States read, "Terrorists' Deadly Attacks Kill Thousands," "Global Economy Suffers," and "Nations Punished Relentlessly by Natural Disasters." The endless stream of negative reporting gave a sense of fear and hopelessness, causing one to wonder if there was any good news to report. Well, God was in control, and He was the good news.

During my trip to Tirupati, 10,035 people made a profession of faith to Jesus Christ as their Savior. Now, that was good news.

Sixteen years spanned the distance between my first and second trips to India. On the second trip, I felt a heavy, oppressive darkness that I had not experienced before.

My place of service was in a militant Hindu area among people who were extremely hostile toward Christians. We were advised to keep a very low profile, as there had been many Christians arrested. Teams that had gone before us had come away frustrated and disillusioned. I vowed to be steadfast and immovable in the strength of God.

Our teams were divided into groups and given our mission. We were all apprehensive about this challenging, hostile environment, but we agreed to press forward. I was teamed up with a local Indian pastor. He was a large man with a booming voice. I was informed that he had been arrested so many times for his boldness in proclaiming the Gospel that the police officers knew him well.

We walked out to get into his SUV, and I was astonished to see in bright orange letters on its sides, JESUS SAVES and JOHN 3:16. So much for being discreet. I thought, *For Him, I'm willing to risk it all, to be totally unrestrained, and to trust in His divine plan.* His plan was soon revealed.

The pastor's unique relationship with the police gave me the chance to proclaim the Gospel inside the prisons, to which government officials had previously denied me access. While in the city, we were under such scrutiny restraining us from sharing that Lazarus and I carried the Good News far out into the villages. We met a local village pastor, who had a fire-burning zeal to preach the Gospel.

The pastor called a village meeting, using me as the bait; all the villagers wanted to see a white man from America. I shared the love and hope of Jesus Christ, and slowly, their cold veneer began to dissipate. Tears flowed down their faces upon hearing about Christ's crucifixion. A thunderous applause resounded upon hearing of His resurrection. The incipient opposition came down like the Jericho wall, and God was in business in the hearts of these villagers.

We traveled to another village where all the men were working in the fields. Fifteen women gathered around, sitting on the dirt to listen to us share God's truth. While I was speaking, I noticed a woman with a strange, distant stare in her eyes. As time went on, she began foaming at the mouth and making sounds like a wounded animal. She shrieked and flopped around like a fish out of water. Lazarus shouted, "She is demon possessed. Cast out the demon, Brother Bee-lee!"

Never in my life had I seen a demon-possessed person. Needless to say, this was totally outside my realm of experience. I walked over to her, grabbed her shoulders, and shouted, "Be gone, in the Name of Jesus Christ!"

Suddenly, she became quiet, limp, and at rest. She lay on the ground as though she was taking a nap. The ladies took her to a hut and cleaned her up. When I saw her later, she had been transformed into a clean, calm, and peaceful woman by the healing power of God.

Another time, I went with Lazarus to his village in Nadikudi. On the two-hour drive over rough terrain from Guntur, Lazarus asked what topic I would be preaching. I had prepared a real "steam winder," as we say in the South. Or so I thought. I told him of my intended topic. He had no response.

We rode in silence for several minutes. Then, this kind, soft-spoken man explained that this area had been suffering from an extreme drought for months. It was imperiling people's health and their very survival. The crops had burned up, cattle were dying from lack of water, and the people were desperate for a message of hope.

He explained that the Hindus had been diligently praying to their gods for rain. He gently asked me to preach a sermon of hope in the Creator and Provider of the rain. It reminded me of the duel between Elijah's God and Baal on Mount Carmel (1 Kings 18:20–40).

As we arrived, hundreds of people were already seated on the ground, waiting for us. I stepped up on the little stage, especially built for me to preach from, and silently asked the Holy Spirit to energize me as I departed from my prepared sermon. Shifting gears, I preached on John 15:7, "If you abide in Me, and I abide in you, you will ask what you desire, and it shall be done for you."

The sun dipped into the west, and I could barely see the audience, but the Holy Spirit's presence was obvious. Just as Lazarus was giving the invitation, a stir rippled through the congregation. I heard screaming and shouting. *What on earth is going on? Has the Holy Spirit fallen on these people? Or is this some kind of satanic attack?* I wondered.

People started running away. Then the frantic screams turned into hysterical laughter. Finally, the mystery was solved. A wild monkey had come to partake of the food people had brought to give as an offering. He scampered through the crowd with a handful of rice and back out into the forest. This was not the atmosphere we had wanted for God's holy moment. I feared that the Spirit had been quenched by this furry distraction.

Our God is a big God, Who handles distractions with ease. He was still present, and holy order was restored; one hundred ninety-five names were added to the Lamb's Book of Life. We concluded the service with a sincere plea to God for rain.

As we drove back to Guntur, it started sprinkling. Moments later, it became a downpour. The drought-stricken area was relieved with three days and nights of abundant rain. The villagers saw this as providential evidence that "the missionaries God" could bring rain even when other gods could not. It was reminiscent of when Nebuchadnezzar declared Daniel's God the Supreme God! (Daniel 4:34–35).

This sweet gift from God had given us unreal credibility. Word of this divine intervention spread like wildfire. We were asked to share God's truth to seventeen more villages.

On one trip, I visited a small village where the homes were made of dry cow dung with thatched roofs. Small children ran around naked or wearing dirty underwear. Some children were rolling old bicycle tires with sticks, while others were kicking cans like soccer balls.

A husband, wife, and their three small children invited me and Lazarus into their hut to share the Gospel. On the floor lay pallets for sleeping. They had a small, low-to-the-ground table to eat on and one straight-backed wooden chair. This was typical of what I saw in other huts.

However, something was very different within this hut. In the corner lounged a six-foot-long cobra. It was round, and firm from its latest meal. The husband told me that he and his family used to be Christians, but now they were snake worshippers.

Lazarus explained to me that this was a common practice in certain villages. At night, the cobras would come out of the forest and enter the huts of the villagers sleeping on the ground. Some believed that keeping a cobra inside their hut kept them safe from other cobras entering unexpectedly. These people, who had barely enough food to feed themselves, fed the snake to pacify it. Then they prayed to the viper, hoping to appease it so it didn't cause harm to the family. This family lived in abject fear of their god, a cobra.

After hearing the story of Jesus, they readily accepted Him as their Savior, but they would not accept Him as the one and only God. We walked away crestfallen as these people lived in deadly fear of their deceitful god but had full access to a loving, protective God.

On a trip to Bangalore, I was accompanied by Margie Whitaker and Rita Shirley, friends from Florida. Bangalore was the fastest-growing city in Asia and is known as the garden city of India. Bangalore is westernized, with favorable conditions, and it is physically less demanding, making this an ideal place for first timers desiring to do missions in India.

While on this trip, I had my first exposure to tribal people. They had their own enclaves and hierarchy. We met with the chief. He explained that a Catholic priest had come and led their ancestors to salvation in Christ fifty years earlier. When the priest left the tribal community, no one was there to teach them or help them to grow spiritually, so they had reverted back to Hinduism. I assured the chief that there was an eager pastor willing to drive three hours each week to disciple them. The entire tribe surrendered its life to Christ.

In Bangalore, I met with thirty-two pastors, training them in the national-to-national program. This vital program for local pastors and laymen trained them how to keep their ministry organized, growing, and effective. We did not want a repetition of what had happened fifty years earlier, leaving a village of new believers without a man of God to help guide them. Training native pastors was far more productive and far less costly than sending someone from the States. It was critical that these new believers were taught in the right way so as not to fall into error, as had the Gnostics in Paul's day.

Preparing to preach one Sunday morning in Nadikudi, my interpreter, Lazarus, asked me to preach on tithing. This was not one of my strong suits or a typical subject for me, but nevertheless, I accepted the challenge. I spoke from Luke 12:34: "For where your treasure is, there your heart will be also."

As is customary, Indian men, women, and children are segregated, and the message had been primarily directed to adults. However, I looked to my right and saw an entire space filled with children. I thought, *Lord, help me to include these children into the sermon.* I concluded by speaking to the children, telling them that their treasure may be a sack of candy or a piece of gum or a shiny marble. I asked if they would be willing to share one of their treasures with God for an offering.

When it came time to receive the offering, which was taken in a sack extended on a long pole, all eyes were on the children's section. One little eight-year-old girl reached into the pocket of her worn dress, separated something from a packet, and placed it into the sack.

We later learned that she gave a piece of gum. But, more important, it was her treasure that she had willingly given to God. Her treasure was in God's hands, and so was her heart.

I have been traveling to India for over thirty years. God has allowed the Billy Gray Ministries to be a blessing to that country in a variety of ways.

John the Baptist is now in charge of the thriving BGM of India, which feeds the poor and teaches Sunday-school classes. He also trains and encourages other pastors to continue fighting the good fight for the Lord.

Lazarus heads an orphanage in Nadikudi, which BGM supports. BGM gave twenty sewing machines for the purpose of training orphan girls so they can earn incomes after departing the orphanage. Indian women volunteers patiently train the girls how to use the machines and instruct in sewing techniques.

BGM has taken over the funding and care of the "Dump Children" orphanage. These are children who were discarded by their parents, literally living in the dump and surviving on refuse. They are now fed, clothed, schooled, and sheltered. Most important, they are taught about the love of Jesus and that they have a Heavenly Father Who will never forsake them.

BGM completed the construction of a hostel that houses a hundred boys, ages five to fourteen. The hostel provides technical training for them to learn a trade. Some will pursue higher education, while others will return to their villages, able to make a living for themselves. (The girls' hostel was built 150 years ago by Southern Baptist but is now run by Australian Baptist.)

While on our trips, we visit and minister to leper colonies, sharing the love of Christ and the purification of His shed blood. Rather than crying out, "unclean, unclean," they now cry out, "Saved by the blood of the Lamb."

We also visit people with AIDS who have been abandoned by family and government, praying with them and sharing Christ's love with them.

BGM has provided medical assistance to thousands—fitting people with glasses, pulling teeth, and treating various illnesses. We have dug wells in far-out villages, providing fresh water from a centrally located source. This prevents villagers from drinking disease-infested water.

BGM has given away countless Bibles, New Testaments, and children's books. We have provided fifty bicycles and one moped for pastors to use for travel, and twenty megaphones for projecting their sermons. BGM has helped incalculable numbers of poor, orphans, widows, and prisoners.

We have trained hundreds of pastors, planted new churches, built churches, and put in cement floors for existing churches with dirt floors.

I have been given the privilege to preach in an immeasurable number of churches, schools, colleges, technical schools, and prisons. I have seen myriads of people saved and baptized.

We do this to share the truth of the life-giving Gospel, not for salvation but because of salvation. It is done in His strength, by His power, and for His glory.

None of these feats can be accomplished without the generous support of the BGM partners, both through prayer and financially. This is a group effort. Without faithful servants of God, I cannot go and spread the Gospel around the world.

Over the past thirty years, not much has changed in Southern India. Some of the roads have been improved, the airports are more modern, and there are a few upscale hotels. But the common folks have not seen much change.

Although we and other ministries see thousands of conversions a year, it does not keep pace with the burgeoning population. We must continue to go share the love of Christ to this country and disciple pastors.

"Wherever He leads, I will go." How about you?

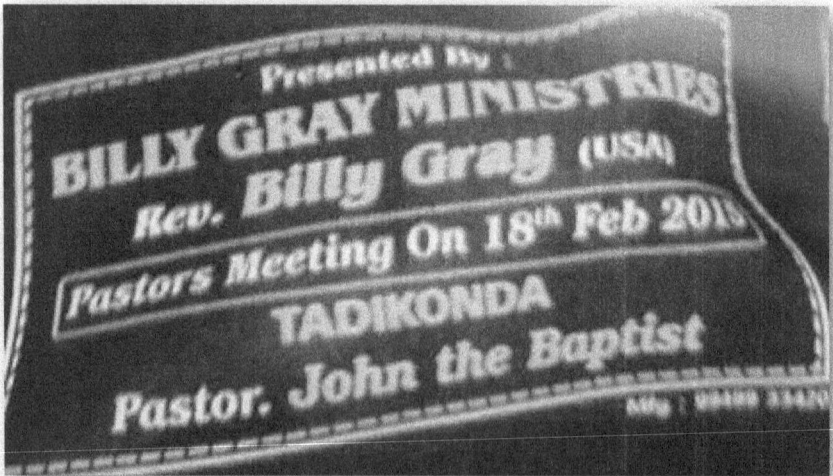

**Briefcase provided
to forty pastors**

CHAPTER 15

News article, Mary Ready

§

BELOW IS AN ARTICLE WRITTEN by Mary Ready of Destin. Published in the Destin Log on February 3, 2009.

THROUGH HEAVEN AND HELL AND BACK AGAIN

Before I read his book, *From Prosecutor to Prison to Preacher*, I only knew him as a nice enough fellow who filled the pulpit when our pastor was absent and liked to tell silly jokes involving Ol' Brother Albert. I also knew him as the dad of Trista, one of the best students I was ever delighted to teach.

So, based on my limited personal knowledge, I would have titled his autobiography, "Funny Preacher Guy, Snappy Dresser, Trista's Dad, and Missionary to Exotic Places." I also knew he was a lawyer at one time, but I liked him anyway.

Then our mutual friend Ms. Betty "Boop" Horton left a copy of his book on my doorstep. "I couldn't let her in because I had the plague at the time." I spent my in-house confinement reading his incredible journey.

In fact, "An Incredible Journey" was a title suggested to him by several friends. But I'm glad he went with the triple "P" alliteration: Prosecutor, prisoner, preacher. What an intriguing trio of words to sum up a man's life, if indeed anyone's life can be summed up that succinctly!

His is a tale of riches to rags to riches once again. But the last pendulum swing brought him wealth of the divine kind. It also has that classic SSS theme: Sin, suffering, and salvation.

The text begins with his trial in Miami and the blood-chilling words, "The United States of America versus Billy Gray." As a prosecutor on staff during the trial of James Earl Ray (accused killer of Martin Luther King Jr.), I'm sure he had heard that sinister pronouncement before. Now, it was directed at him, and the message was clear: "Yes, all the people in the United States are personally offended by you."

I won't go into more detail in case you want to read the book. So, I'll just skip past the charges, the conviction, and the years of federal incarceration, to the mostly happy ending.

Billy Gray now lives in Destin.

His children, Ty and Trista have given him three beautiful grandchildren, Erika, Hannah and Caleb. Sadly, his wife Pat, a registered nurse, high school teacher and successful business woman died of cancer in 1992.

Shortly after her mom's death, Trista sent me a copy of the eulogy she had written in Pat's memory. She wanted me to critique the poem, but this tough old English teacher, so used to wielding the red pen upon student work, was too touched by a daughter's heartbroken love to find even a comma out of place.

Currently, Brother Billy makes three to five mission trips yearly to places across five continents, although his heart may belong to India, where his ministry is the major support for an orphanage. He has kept his promise to God made in a prison chapel when, driven to his knees, he confessed his sin, acknowledged Him as Savior, and vowed to "be His man." If God would give him the opportunity to speak as His representative, then he would make better use of the gift that had made him a formidable attorney. Only this time, he would be an advocate in the highest court of all.

Nearly thirty years later, only his Redeemer knows the actual number of souls he has touched and the great good he has done worldwide. I can't think of anyone more deserving of an "atta boy" from Jesus or a "Well done, good and faithful servant."

However, I'm sure he would modestly disagree.

Like Christian, the main character in John Bunyan's "Pilgrim's Progress," Billy Gray's journey serves God's purpose. His twisting path has taken him from privilege and pride, to the pit of prison, to patient preacher of the Gospel.

Truth be told, any one of us could be the central character in our own "Pilgrim's Progress" since we (like sheep who've gone astray) can tell our own tales of sin and self-destruction.

We can only hope—as in Brother Billy's example—that the path of our journey leads to restored fellowship with the One Who is the Author of all our stories.

CHAPTER 16

News article, David Duvall

§

BELOW IS AN ARTICLE WRITTEN by Pastor David Duvall of Niceville, Florida. Published in the Destin Log on May 15, 2010.

FAITHFULNESS IS THE HIGHEST OF CHRISTIAN CALLINGS

There was a story that I remember reading when I was young called *The Faithful Gray*. It was about a gray horse who was ever so faithful to his master. The story told of how the horse performed such acts as carrying his master to town far away when he was sick even though he himself was very ill.

The horse also braved a barn fire to pull his owner to safety even though horses are petrified of fire. The story included many other brave and faithful acts.

The Bible tells us that faithfulness is one of the nine fruits of the Spirit that we are to exemplify. Faithfulness as mentioned in the passage of Galatians 5:22–23 describes the characteristics of one who has integrity and is trustworthy, one who can be depended on.

In other passages (Luke 16:10–12; Titus 2:10) the word "faithful" is used to describe a committed, trustworthy servant of God who will do what he is supposed to do.

One instruction that Jesus has given us is to be faithful not only to him but to one another as brothers and sisters in Christ. In the book of Colossians, found in the New Testament of the Bible, the apostle Paul, the author, mentions three men whom he refers to as faithful men of the ministry. The first was a man named Epaphras who was a native to Colossae in Asia and was commissioned by Paul to preach. He also worked hard for the churches in Laodicea and Hierapolis and then later was imprisoned with Paul in Rome. Paul refers to him as a servant of Jesus Christ, a title Paul gives to only two other people besides himself. The others were Timothy and a man named Tychicus. Tychicus is the second man Paul mentions here in Colossians as being faithful. This man was a traveling companion of Paul on his third missionary journey and he also served as a substitute preacher and then a courier of Paul's letters.

Onesimus is also mentioned as a man of integrity and faithfulness. He had been a slave who came to know Jesus after escaping and then became a trusted friend and help to Paul.

I bring up these three men because they are not well known, predominate Bible characters. They were not famous nor did they hold high positions or high rank, but they were faithful men and friends whom Paul thought of enough to write about as examples to those in the church at the day and even to us in today's churches.

General Dwight D. Eisenhower once rebuked one of his generals for referring to a soldier as "just a private." He reminded him that the army could function better without its generals than it could without its foot soldiers. If this war is won," he said, "it will be won by privates."

In the same way the common, ordinary, one-talent Christians are the very backbone of the church. We have our great evangelists, our super congregations led by dynamic elders, and our wealthy brethren who are able to finance great works. But, if the work of the Lord is to be done, if the Gospel is to be taken to the lost, if encouragement and faithfulness is to be exemplified, it will be done by the so-called ordinary Christians.

I know of another story of a faithful Gray, who is not a horse, but a man no book has written about. He is not a world-famous evangelist although he has preached the Gospel to thousands in other countries of the world. He is not pastor of a large church although he has the capabilities and character to be.

His name, Billy Gray, always brings back the memory to me of that horse who was so faithful to his master. Billy has not only been faithful to his Master who is Jesus, but he has also been a faithful friend and encourager to me.

Just as the names of those three men from Paul's writings mentioned earlier were not bell ringers to most of you, the name Billy Gray may not be either. However, he is one whom Paul would surely name as faithful and true, a servant of Christ. He is an ordinary man who taught me in Sunday school for some years and although we are somewhat separated by age, economic status, and intelligence, he has always encouraged, inspired, and befriended me. Even when I attended another class for a while, he still called and checked in on me. Though I have gone on to pastor at a different church, he still has been a faithful friend, a man of integrity and love.

You, too, can be found faithful to the Lord and to others whether you are ordinary in man's eyes or a well-known citizen or preacher. Is there someone who needs you to be faithful to them as a brother or sister in Christ? When we are faithful friends to one another, we are also found faithful to the Lord in many ways.

Billy, the faithful Gray! Sounds like a good title for a book on Christian character.

COMMENTS

§

Everything Billy Gray does in this life is with the kingdom in mind. From talking with a server at a local restaurant to traveling the world, Billy is passionate about wanting everyone to know Jesus. He is a master story-teller and finds humor in all sorts of situations. This book is a delight and an encouragement for the reader.

~ Sherry Leavell

Billy has a way of doing what all of us want to do. We want to be used by God in any circumstance. Most of us, though, have our ideas of what God should be doing through us. Therefore, we already have a plan, and we tend to not follow the lead of our Lord. I give thanks for Billy and others who lead by example by simply being an instrument to be used by the Almighty. Obedience really is that simple.

~Richard Hetzel

I have been blessed to know both Brother Gray and his precious daughter, Trista. I served with him as a fellow worshipper in a local church and taught Trista in her Senior year of high school. No two sweeter witnesses for our Lord have I ever met.

~Mary Ready

My wife and I were privileged to go on a mission trip with Billy Gray and just witnessing his commitment to spreading Gods word to lost folks gave us the energy and drive to share with as many people that we could find. Billy has become a great friend to the two of us and he has helped me work through some tough issues in the managing of an organization. We thank God for putting Billy Gray in our lives and look forward to our next project together.

~Rick Pauly

www.ingramcontent.com/pod-product-compliance
Lightning Source LLC
Chambersburg PA
CBHW071002040426
42443CB00007B/620